The Role of Transportation in Regional Economic Development

Charles River Associates Incorporated is a professional service organization in Cambridge, Massachusetts, that specializes in economic and econometric research. CRA has conducted research in the fields of transportation, pollution control and abatement, and natural resource industries, among others. CRA's work is generally performed for long-range planning and policy formulating groups in industry and government.

CRA

The Role of Transportation in Regional Economic Development

A Charles River Associates Research Study

Gerald Kraft
John R. Meyer
Jean-Paul Valette

Lexington Books
D.C. Heath and Company
Lexington, Massachusetts
Toronto   London

Published simultaneously in Canada.

Printed in the United States of America.

International Standard Book Number: 0-669-62410-0

Library of Congress Catalog Card Number: 72-158829

Table of Contents

List of Figures and Tables

Figure

Table

Preface

This book is based on a study performed in 1966 by the authors for Charles River Associates, Cambridge, Massachusetts. That study was done under contract to the Office of Regional and Economic Development (ORED) of the U.S. Department of Commerce.

As commissioned by ORED, the authors investigated the extent to which economists have been able to identify and measure the impact of transportation in regional economic development. As performed, the study became a state-of-the-art report of both the theoretical and empirical work that has been done in the field.

During the course of the study the authors consulted with many specialists and experts in regional and transportation economics, whose assistance was invaluable. Particular thanks should be expressed to James R. Nelson, for his useful comments during the first phase of the study; Kiochi Mera, who provided a great deal of information during the writing of Chapters 2, 3, and 4; Daniel Shimshoni, whose knowledge of transportation technology was helpful in preparing Chapter 5; Martin L. Lindahl, who wrote the first draft of Chapter 6; and Martin Wohl, whose grasp of the problems of urban transportation provided the basis for the writing of Chapter 7.

Special appreciation and thanks should be expressed to David L. McNicol for his overall contribution to the research, writing, and editing of the final report and for his careful annotation of the bibliography.

The contents of this book reflect solely the views of the authors, who take full responsibility for the conclusions presented. The work of writing this book was a mutual effort of all three authors, and reflects an equal amount of their time, thought, and judgment. Accordingly the order of authorship was set alphabetically.

**The Role of
Transportation
in Regional
Economic
Development**

1 Introduction

Scope and Objectives

In the economic literature, it has become axiomatic to say that growth and the momentum at which it occurs depend, among other things, on geography and location of activities. Within a nation, the development of a region is directly related to its ease of access to resources and to outside markets, or more generally to its physical position relative to other regions. Transportation systems are designed to overcome the frictions (distances, natural obstacles, etc.) imposed by geography. As such, they shape the distribution of activities and influence the share by which each region contributes to the national product.

The purpose of this study is to determine to what extent economists have answered the question of whether, how and by how much transportation affects regional development. In the context of the U.S. economy, characterized admittedly by an extensively developed transportation system, it is also relevant to investigate the extent to which marginal adaptations in the system may help economically retarded regions to develop and to attract activities in which their participation has been historically low.

In order to lend itself to practical conclusions, or at least lead to meaningful results, the analysis should also evaluate the merits of the theory in view of past experience and current trends. Needless to say, the lessons of the past do not provide perfect guidelines for the future. History has taught us that events rarely repeat themselves exactly, because of the elusive nature of the forces which provoke them. Similarly, transportation is not an isolated phenomenon; its impact is enhanced by the interaction of a variety of other economic stimuli whose magnitude cannot be predicted with great certainty. While the findings of this study may show some of the effect that transportation had on the profile of regions and permit an anticipation of the future role of transportation, they should be interpreted more as trends and tendencies than as absolute predictions.

Outline of the Study

Chapter 2 describes various theoretical attempts to explain the role of transportation in regional development, with particular emphasis on interregional transportation, not because of its importance but because it is this type of transportation which has received the greatest attention in the economics litera-

1

ture. In Chapter 3, the validity of the theories as predictive tools is evaluated by
investigating the empirical evidence of geographical shifts in the industrial
structure of this country. On this basis, certain conclusions are derived with
respect to the role that transportation may play in the future. Chapter 4 analyzes
modes and modal characteristics. Chapter 5 investigates the historical impact of
rate-making procedures on the development of some regions, while Chapter 6
catalogs and evaluates the significance of innovations that appear on the horizon.
Finally, Chapter 7 discusses the role of urban transportation in development
programs.

Sources: Theoretical Analyses and Empirical Studies

The relationship between transportation and growth is suggested in different
aspects of economic theory, especially trade theory, location theory, development economics and regional economics; to a lesser degree, it has also been
treated by welfare economists, geographers, city planners and highway engineers.

With various degrees of emphasis, economists have recognized that a major
impetus for growth comes, at least in the short run, from the ability of a region
to produce goods and services demanded by the national economy and to market
these at a competitive advantage with respect to other regions. This propensity to
export obviously depends to some extent on the access that a region has to outside markets both for its inputs and its outputs; it is also related to the efficiency
that a region shows in assembling its factors of production, and depends therefore on the internal economic structure of the region. In the long run, growth
becomes more self-sustaining when a region can achieve sizeable regional markets
for activities other than those oriented directly toward export.

Once analytical significance and practical content is given to the concept of
a region, it becomes clear that transportation facilities, by linking consumption
and production centers within and outside the region, play a distinct role in
conditioning the pattern of growth. Trade and location theorists, who generally
consider a region as a grouping of activities on a map, have implicitly recognized
this. For example, the interregional programming techniques elaborated by
trade economists and by transportation engineers are based on this approach.
More generally, transportation, by connecting the regions, develops regional resources on the basis of interregional comparative advantage. This is a condition
for efficiency at the national (aggregate) level. In Chapter 2 a discussion is presented of how interregional transportation contributes to national as well as
regional welfare by permitting each region to develop its economic base.

For regional economists the function of transportation extends beyond the
mere interregional exchange of commodities and services. Good interregional
connections facilitate the convergence of the factors of production, labor in particular, toward the centers of production. They contribute to the geographical
concentration of activities originating in the advantages of large-scale production

and help the cumulative process by which cities grow. Conversely, they may relieve cities by inviting congested industries to disperse. Finally, the development of an extensive internal transportation network permits regions to achieve sizeable internal markets, by integrating subregions into larger geographical units.

Inter- and Intraregional Transportation

A distinction which facilitates the appraisal of the role of transportation within regional development programs, can be drawn between the inter- and intraregional functions of transportation. Admittedly, this distinction may be somewhat artificial. The roads along which the interregional flows of commodities are channeled are often the same as those which permit the movements of people between residence and job location. A highway system very often performs simultaneously all the functions which have been assigned by regional economists to transportation. On the other hand, air, rail, and water transportation, because of the heavy terminal costs which characterize these modes, have been traditionally, at least to date, oriented toward long distance, interregional flows of commodities and passengers. The distinction is therefore not a mere abstraction; it has the concrete support of traffic specialization created by technological differentials between modes.

Another obstacle to a clear-cut distinction between intra- and interregional transportation results from the absence of permanent and clear-cut delineations between regions. There are no actual regions which meet simultaneously all criteria by which economists have conceptualized ideal regions. Depending upon the desired degree of homogeneity, the nature and number of homogeneous characteristics which a region must present, or simply on the economic objectives of the planner, interregional boundaries will change, and so will the interpretation to be given to interregional transportation. This is reflected in the way different government agencies have set regional boundaries. For example, the Ozarks Region, designated for federal assistance under the Economic Development Act of 1965, cuts across the South and North Central Regions commonly used as basic regions by the Bureau of the Census. Thus, while the Little Rock-New Orleans axis would be considered as an interregional link under EDA specifications, the same line is clearly an intraregional connection for the Bureau of the Census.

Finally, because of the special situation of cities, both inter- and intraregional transportation functions are often integrated in urban networks. In support of the trading activity of the city, transportation is geared toward the movement of commodities (industrial sectors) and of people (service sectors). The city serves as a switchboard between the national system along which interregional flows of goods and people occur, and the feeder lines channeling those flows within the region.

National vs. Regional Impact of Transportation

Traditionally, economists have assigned a major role to transportation programs in the drive of nations for economic expansion. Transportation facilities
overcome the frictions of space and the obstacles which geography poses to the
optimal utilization of resources. Under such a goal, funds should be allocated to
those portions of the transportation system which, to at least a first approximation, contribute most to growth of national product. In essence, this means that
transportation expenditures should be distributed geographically so that production will be attracted to locations where economic activity is most profitable. In
anticipation of what will be amplified in later sections, we can say that such a
policy tends to reinforce interregional specialization of activities along lines of
static comparative advantage.

Thus, when policy makers focus their attention on national growth, they do
so without regard to where growth occurs. Regional growth as such is a subordinated objective. With the emphasis on national growth, some regions will
grow, of course, and others may not. By definition, however, if national growth
is maximized, total regional growth should more than compensate any potential
regional losses.

By contrast, it can be argued that growth of a particular region is not necessarily or obviously accompanied by a net gain to the nation. This is, of course, a
potent argument against a regional approach to evaluating transport investments;
it might also explain the apparent lack of attention to the theoretical relationship between transportation expenditures and regional development.

For example, the possibility of a dichotomy between policies based on
regional or national growth objectives is illustrated by the difficulties which Soviet
planners confronted in the 1930s and 1940s. Extension of the Soviet rail system
was designed precisely to "regionalize" industries and increase the participation
of eastern territories in the national product. The facts show that the shift toward
the East in fact did not live up to the expectations of the Soviet officials. Rapid
industrial growth conflicted with a more scattered dispersion of economic activities so it became expedient to reinforce the transportation network around the
established production centers of the West.

The experience of the USSR should not be interpreted too literally; in the
context of the U.S. economy, the concentration of social overhead expenditures
in the most developed areas would correspond to a narrow application of the
marginalist doctrine of product maximization, which is, in any case, too static
to encompass the reality of development. For several reasons, transportation-
induced regional growth is not necessarily incompatible with a rapid national
expansion, particularly in the long run.

For example, the private decisions that shape the patterns of economic
development in a market economy, such as that of the United States, may not
lead unambiguously to maximization of national income or other broad economic

aggregates. For one thing, serious imperfections may exist in many markets so that the private calculus deviates significantly from a more comprehensive social calculus of gain. Imperfections in capital markets are perhaps most commonly cited in this regard. Labor market imperfections, particularly in the form of labor immobility, may also be prevalent. In general, an underlying rationale of many regional redevelopment programs in Western Europe and North America is the notion that private market decisions may not be making optimal use of all of the resources in a country. In particular, if social benefits and costs are counted carefully, the marginal return from directing investment toward certain regions which might otherwise be neglected may augment the marginal returns realized nationally on capital accumulations.

Furthermore, in developed countries which have already achieved high per capita incomes, some deemphasis on growth of aggregate national income might be accepted for the benefit of regional development objectives, on simple welfare or redistributive grounds.

Similarly, inefficient transportation policies may have historically distorted the optimal distribution of activities and retarded the development of otherwise well-endowed regions. A related argument is that the overextension of transportation networks in some regions has hampered the normal rate of growth of other regions. The opinion has been expressed, for instance, that during the 1940s the South did not keep pace with the rest of the country because of a transportation lag.[1] Similarly, a study has associated the drop in manufacturing employment in West Virginia in the early 1950s with the fact that the state had merely maintained its transportation system while the adjacent states were developing modern networks.[2] This emphasizes the dynamic relationship which exists between the networks of the various regions of a country.

Finally, the absence of adequate transportation may constitute a major bottleneck to the exploitation of natural resources. Although the ubiquity of the U.S. trunk system seems to minimize the potential importance of this factor for the development of physically exportable resources in the United States, the development of transportation may permit a larger exploitation of such immobile resources as landscape and climate.

---

1. Calvin B. Hoover and B. U. Ratchford, *Economic Resources and Policies of the South* (London: Macmillan, 1951), p. 338.

2. Bertram H. Lindman, "Proposed Interstate Highway, Great Lakes to Florida," an economic report to the West Virginia State Road Commission, 1956.

The Theory of Transportation and Development

Preliminary Remarks

Transportation theory has limited applicability to explaining regional development in the United States. This failure cannot be attributed to a logical flaw in the theory itself, but rather to the unrealism or oversimplification of its assumptions and to the irrelevance of the problems which it intends to solve. The following paragraphs list (not necessarily in order of importance) reasons which explain this limited applicability of the theory to the regional growth problems of the United States.

A first set of limitations revolves around the aspect that underdevelopment assumes in the United States. To a large extent, the theory aims at finding the transportation system which will achieve an optimum development of resources within an area; it applies, therefore, to situations where resources exist and where transportation facilities are lacking. The depressed regions of the United States are often typical of the opposite situation where the transportation network is adequate but the resources are vanishing or losing their economic value. Such is the case for instance, in West Virginia which has good railroads but where coal, as a resource, is losing ground. In general, the U.S. transportation system is characterized by over- rather than under-capacity. In many instances, the problem of transportation is not to extend the system but to "manage" it, by imposing an efficient rate structure and adapting its technological characteristics to an ever-changing demand. While theory assigns a positive role to transportation in the course of economic expansion by redistributing economic activities, it is generally admitted that in the United States today, "changes in industrial output and in location appear to alter the structure of transportation rather than the converse"[1] (e.g., because of the diminishing transportation component in sales price).

Other difficulties evolve from the fact that the available theory is essentially static in the sense that it analyzes the shifts in industrial location resulting from changes in processing and transportation costs at one instant in time. In reality, the relocation of industry responds also to changes in production technology, to the emergence or the destruction of resources or to changes in the composition of the national demand, which are the dynamic characteristics of a progressive

---

1. Marion J. Barloon, "The Interrelationship of the Changing Structure of American Transportation and Changes in Industrial Location," *Land Economics*, Vol. XLI, No. 2 (May, 1965) pp. 169–179.

economy. Such elements may ultimately be so strong as to annihilate the locational impact of a transportation program. While economists recognize that such factors exist, they are still in the process of developing the conceptual tools which could incorporate them in computationally feasible models.

In a developed economy, moreover, transportation service has many dimensions which vary in importance for different industries. In fulfilling the transportation demand of the industries which a region can attract, policy makers are, therefore, faced with a crucial selection among technologically different modes. Typically, a transportation service which can be bought with a fixed budget is represented in terms of ton miles, at a certain speed, with a given waiting time, and with a certain probability of damage. Depending on its nature, an industry may be attracted to a region which offers fast service at a high cost rather than slow service at a low cost. Premium transportation thus may take preference over cheap transportation. As a corollary, choice of mode usually must take future transportation innovations into consideration. In general, available knowledge about the factors which enter into the actual location decision of the entrepreneur is too limited to assess the effectiveness of a given relative transportation advantage.

The Theory

The theoretical relationship between transportation and regional economic development can be derived from two somewhat related applications of international trade theory. The first one expresses the idea that the growth of a region is directly dependent on the strength of its exchanges with other regions and rests on the concept of the international trade multiplier. This aspect of the doctrine reveals little of the relationship between changes in transportation and shifts in interregional flow; however, once those are known, it permits us to measure the impact of such shifts on a regional economy. The second application refers to the fusion of trade and location theories and permits an analysis of the mechanism of interregional flows of goods and commodities when the transportation cost structure is considered as a variable.

Base Theory: A Primitive Multiplier Doctrine.

Economic base theory may be considered as the first element of a theory of transportation and development. In its original formulation the doctrine says that the growth of a small area is directly determined by its ability to market its products and services outside its boundaries. During the 1930s Hoyt thought the ability of a city to sustain its economic activity depends on its ability to export goods and services to the rest of the world. He also thought that the total size of the economic activities of a city is a constant multiple of the export sector, implying a unit of export activity generates a certain number of activities which are dependent upon and serving the export activity. Therefore, it was reasoned that the only way to expand the size of the economy is to expand the export sector. Being called the economic base theory, this theory prevailed among city planners until the 1950s, when Andrews and Blumenfeld critically reviewed the underlying concepts.[2]

Blumenfeld specifically challenged the causative assumption that it is the export sector that determines the economy as a whole. He argued that what determines the export sector is the city or region's competitive position vis-à-vis other cities and regions, and what determines the competitive position of a city or region is the quality of the service sector. Therefore, he argued that what determines the economy as a whole is the service sector but not the basic or export sector. In the mid-1950s Tiebout extended Blumenfeld's argument by adding that the quality of the service sector may determine the quantity of the export sector and that the quantity of the export sector helps determine the quality of the service sector. Therefore, Blumenfeld's arguments may not necessarily contradict base theory, but rather complement it.

Under a strict application of base theory, the role of transportation can be described but not economically evaluated; essentially it consists of providing the interregional geographical linkages on which the flows of export goods will be channeled. Viewed in this perspective, the demand for transport facilities is obviously a derived demand, and it is the nature of the basic sector which determines the geographical direction of the transportation links (from production centers to markets) and also the appropriate selection and coordination of technologically different modes. Commodities or services have specific shipping characteristics, such as weight, volume, divisibility, and perishability, to which one mode or a specific combination of modes will be best adapted. An important aspect of planning consists, therefore, of fitting technological mode characteristics (capacity, number of transfers, size of containers , speed, etc.) to the shipping characteristics of the products. All this however is not very relevant until transportation is analyzed in terms of costs, which cannot be done in the framework of the base doctrine. The base theory is limited, in general, by its descriptive rather than analytical nature. An inherent weakness of the base doctrine is that its validity, both as an historical explanation of regional expansion and as a conceptual tool for implementing development programs, dwindles when the sizes of regions increase. Finally, the base theory has little application to the problems of an underdeveloped region which is characterized, among other things, by a seeming inability to develop an export base.

---

2. Richard B. Andrews, "Mechanics of the Urban Economic Base," a series of articles in *Land Economics*, Vol. 29 through 31 (May, 1953 to February, 1956). Hans Blumenfeld, "The Economic Base of the Metropolis," *Journal of the American Institute of Planners*, Vol. 21, No. 4 (Fall, 1955).

Multiplier Analysis and Input-Output Models.

1. The Doctrine.   Assuming, as will be established later, that changes in transportation structure affect the demand for a region's products, multiplier analysis states that the exports of a region may generate a succession of economic impulses which increase economic activity in the region by far more than the original value of the exports, and that the total activity generated depends to a certain extent on the industrial structure of the region.

When regional income is increased by a certain amount from an external source, such as exports to another region, the increased amount will be divided by the recipients within the regions into consumption and savings, but the increased savings are not necessarily channeled to investment. Therefore, the aggregate effective demand may lag behind its "full" potential. However, the increased consumption necessarily increases demand by the same amount, and that increased effective demand, in turn, generates another round of income, and so forth. The process continues until the increase in the aggregate peters out through successive "leakages" of the increased incomes to savings. As a result the original amount of exogenous payment is magnified by a multiplicative factor m related to the marginal propensity to consume, *MPC* in the formula

$$m = \frac{1}{1 - MPC}. \tag{1}$$

For example, if two-thirds of a payment received by an individual in a region is used for consumption, then an export dollar should eventually generate \$3.00 in total income payments in the region.

Obviously, the above formula applies only in the case of an entirely self-sufficient economy, because of the two-way direction of interregional exchanges. Since the increase of consumption demand of a region can be met by supplies from other regions (regional imports), the income stream generated within a region by a given amount of export is equal to that amount times m where

$$m = \frac{1}{1 - (MPC - MPI)}, \tag{2}$$

MPI being the propensity to import.

A region, therefore, will be able to capitalize on its exports to the extent that the income generated is retained within the region. The magnitude of the marginal propensity to import varies, depending upon the size and the structure of the regional economy; the more the regional economy is self-sufficient (through larger size or more diversification), the less the marginal propensity to import.

There is, of course, very little that transportation can do to increase the general propensity to consume, *MPC*, but there may be much it can do to increase the propensity to consume within the region (*MPC* – *MPI*), at least in theory. For example, it is recognized that for consumer goods any decrease of short-haul costs tends to favor the local producer, over the long distance producer, or, what amounts to the same thing, possibly attracts the latter to the region.

2. Input-Output Techniques. Input-output traces how a stimulus of external origin, such as an increase in exports, is propagated throughout an economy. Because of the technological and geographical links which exist in the economy, the input-output matrix requires a disaggregation of the economy into industrial sectors or into regions, or into both. In its ideal form, an input-output matrix would contain a considerable number of elements, each one representing the trade relationship of a particular regional industry to all other regional industries in the economy.[3] This ideal form is not realized in practice, either because of lack of data or because of certain elements which are not necessary to the solution of a problem. Depending upon the nature of a particular problem, data simplifications consisting of certain intersectoral or interregional aggregations are often made.

It is not useful here to review the history of input-output models, except by mentioning the early and the latest efforts in this field. Goodwin pioneered the multiplier concept, using an input-output matrix developed earlier by Leontief.[4] The regional dimension (which was not explicitly accounted for by Goodwin) was introduced by Metzler.[5] A few years later Leontief and Isard published an analysis of regions using input-output techniques.[6] By 1955 the use of the input-output technique for prediction of interregional short-run impacts were conceptually completed by Moore.[7] The technique has been applied more recently by Bolton[8] to analyze the regional aspects of federal expenditures for defense.

---

3. For a simple text book explanation, see W. Miernyk *The Elements of Input-Output Analysis* (New York: Random House, 1957).

4. R. M. Goodwin, "The Multiplier as Matrix," *Economic Journal*, Vol. 59, No. 236 (Dec., 1949).

5. L. A. Metzler, "A Multiple Region Theory of Increase and Trade," *Econometrica*, Vol. 18, No. 4 (Oct., 1950).

6. Walter Isard, "Some Empirical Results and Problems of Regional Input-Output Analysis," in W. Leontief, ed. *Studies in the Structure of the American Economy* (New York: Oxford University Press, 1953).

7. F. T. Moore, "Regional Economic Reaction Paths," *American Economic Review*, Vol. 45, No. 2 (May, 1955).

8. Roger E. Bolton, *Defense Purchases and Regional Growth*, (Washington, Brookings Institution, 1966). See also Wassily Leontief, et. al., "The Economic Impact – Industrial and Regional – of an Arms Cut," *Review of Economics and Statistics*, Vol. 48, No. 3 (August, 1965).

Trade Theory

Once it is recognized that trade patterns and the geographical distribution of
activities mutually determine each other, there would be no reason to treat trade
and location theory separately. Before being merged, both disciplines have,
however, followed different historical paths, and some specific contributions of
location theory, such as the focus on agglomeration factors as a locational element,
have not been completely integrated into trade models. Agglomeration factors
may be defined as the economic benefits received by a firm from clustering with
other firms.

Trade economists have given empirical meaning to the concept of the export
base by identifying the conditions under which movements of goods occur between regions. They have also explicitly recognized the role of transportation
costs in such trade patterns. Trade theory's fundamental theorem was enunciated
by Ricardo[9] in the early part of the nineteenth century, and applied to interregional trade by Ohlin.[10]

Ricardo's model is simple: it involves two nations (regions) and two commodities. Briefly stated, the theory states that two areas will exchange the commodities in which they have a *comparative* advantage. In a strict international
framework, comparative advantage refers to the *relatively* greater efficiency that
one nation has over another in producing a commodity when the price of such
commodity is expressed in terms of the other commodities that a nation can
manufacture. In the interregional context, comparative advantage implies the existence of *absolute* price differentials between different locations. The theoretical
distinction between the international and interregional situation is not terribly
significant here since it does not invalidate the basic conclusion that trade spurs
the territorial division of labor or, in other words, the regional specialization of
economic activities.

Once transportation costs are introduced into trade theory, the relationship
between transportation and growth can be analyzed, and most theorems of location theory can be derived. The distinction between trade and location theory
depends almost solely on the way one looks at transportation costs as determinants of either location or of commodity flows.

In its present form trade theory places the concept of comparative advantage
in a system of geographical coordinates and considers interregional trade as resulting from price differentials that exist at the market place. What determines the
volume and direction of a region's exchanges is, therefore, its efficiency in manufacturing and distributing its goods at an advantage over other regions. Comparative advantage should, therefore, be considered the resulting force of two

---

9. David Ricardo, *Principles of Political Economy and Taxation* (Homewood, Ill.:
Richard D. Irwin, 1963; original, 1817).

10. Bertil Ohlin, *Interregional and International Trade* (Cambridge: Harvard University
Press, 1933).

components: a production advantage and a transportation advantage. Trade models have analyzed, with various degrees of sophistication, the interplay between these two elements. Conceptually, the superimposition of transportation differentials over production differentials will tend to specialize a region, say i, in those activities for which

$$P_i + T_i < P_j + T_j , \tag{3}$$

or
$$P_i < P_j + (T_j - T_i) , \tag{4}$$

or
$$P_i - P_j < T_j - T_i ; \tag{5}$$

where P_i and P_j represent costs of production in regions i and j and T_i and T_j represent transportation costs from regions i and j to the market place.

In the absence of transportation costs, each region would specialize in the production of the commodities for which $P_i < P_j$. In the classical model, the existence of differentials in resource endowments creates interregional price differences. While exchanges are stimulated by such price differences, they can be offset by the existence of high transportation costs. In that sense space creates frictions, and imposes a barrier on interregional trade very much as a tariff does in international trade.

The nature of regional specialization is dependent on the cost structure of the interregional transportation system. It is clear from inequality (5) that a transportation advantage or disadvantage $(T_j - T_i)$ can reinforce, cancel out, or reverse a production advantage $(P_i - P_j)$. To put it another way, the role of transportation in economic development consists of providing a region with an economic advantage relative to other regions, enabling it to secure a larger share of the national demand for certain products.

Some general conclusions on the effect of changes in transportation costs on the interregional distribution of activities, can be illustrated by a simple example, as in Figure 2-1. Say that a country consists of three regions, I, II and III. With respect to a particular commodity, oranges, for instance, two of the regions are in a situation where they can produce this commodity, the third region being the consumer of oranges. Regions I and II can grow oranges at A and B, respectively, at costs of $10 and $6. Clearly, Region II (which, we might assume, has the same spatial relationship to Region III as Region I) has an advantage in growing oranges. For both regions, assume that the trunk lines connecting the producing centers to the market are archaic, and are characterized by high transportation costs. Further assume that it costs $8 to move oranges from B to M and $5 from A to M (although in straight line AM = BM). Although the BM line is more inefficient than AM, this inefficiency is more than overcome by the price differential between A and B (so that Region II will specialize in orange growing, since at the market, its products will sell at a lower price, 14, as opposed to 15 for products

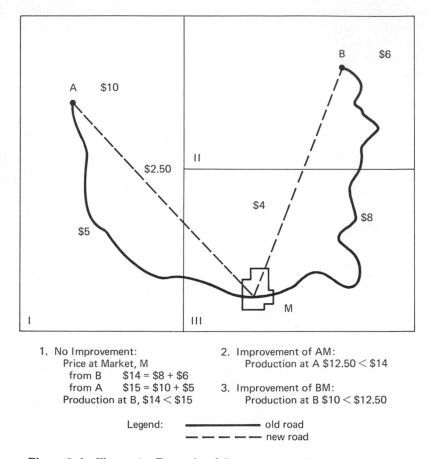

1. No Improvement: 2. Improvement of AM:
       Price at Market, M   Production at A $12.50 < $14
       from B $14 = $8 + $6
       from A $15 = $10 + $5   3. Improvement of BM:
    Production at B, $14 < $15   Production at B $10 < $12.50

              Legend: ——————— old road
                               — — — — — new road

Figure 2–1. Illustrative Example of Comparative Advantage.

of Region I. It is, however, possible for Region I to improve its system and to establish a more direct trunk line, which would, for instance, cut transportation costs by half. In that case, the advantage of Region II has been destroyed and A will now grow oranges since at the market its products are cheaper (12.5 vs. 14). This is true only if Region II does not retaliate, by also establishing a more direct line. In that case, Region II would regain its advantage (10 vs. 12.5).

This fairly unsophisticated example permits the derivation of some important conclusions which are important in analyzing the effects of a transportation system linking regions:

1. The effect of a *general* decrease in transportation costs is to give greater locational influence to production cost differentials between regions. While carrying well-endowed regions and the nation in general to new peaks of

affluence and material progress, the resulting specialization trend may by-pass resource-poor regions. Improvement of interregional links in general may act against rather than for the depressed regions if those areas do not have the resources necessary to acquire an absolute advantage in at least one commodity. Economic retardation is, therefore, not necessarily connected with inadequacy of the transportation network.

2. Improvement in the trunk system of a particular region might shift comparative advantage between regions. However, a transportation advantage is not a perfect substitute for a natural production cost advantage in the sense that the corresponding transportation cost differentials are normally less permanent than interregional production cost differentials which are based, say, on resource endowments. Endowing a region with good trunk lines might help it to capture outside markets from other regions which have a superior resource base, but only as long as the other regions do not retaliate by improving their own trunk lines. Strategies with respect to transportation development must, therefore, be analyzed in a dynamic and overall systems context.

3. The case for transportation as a substitute for comparative advantage should not be overstated. In our example, we can see that whatever improvement Region I may make in its transportation system, it will not be able to supply the market if its costs of growing oranges are greater than 14.

4. Details are needed on the factors that create a transportation advantage. In our example, the lowering of transport costs between A and M was achieved by developing a straight trunk line; in other words, by the altering of the distance relationship between the two points. A similar result would have been obtained in theory by a modification of the rate structure. Whether this is feasible involves complex questions on both cost and revenue sides. Lower transportation costs might also result from changes in the technology of the transport system. A region usually specializes in several export commodities, all of which have the same basic transportability properties (density, weight, value, perishability, etc.). Because these properties vary in degree from one commodity to the other, shippers rank differently the basic attributes of any transportation mode, which may consist for instance of speed, regularity of service, waiting time, and probability of damage and loss. For a particular transportation service, i.e., an identical bundle of the above characteristics, different transportation modes are offered at different prices, and the shipper's choice will probably be to use the cheapest. For example, the transportation of lumber requires a low level of the four modal characteristics described above; although lumber may be carried by air, road, water and rail, it will be generally transported over long distances by rail or water which offer the cheapest combination of the mode characteristics at the level required. For the same reasons, cut flowers will be transported by air. Cheapness of a particular mode is not absolute but depends on the type of

transportation service which is required. Mode selection is relatively easy when the regional product is homogeneous, but can become very complex in the case of a diversified product.

5.   A transportation network channels commodity flow in two directions, from a region toward national markets and vice-versa. Because of this, a transportation development program is a two-edged weapon in regional development. Obviously, the net impact depends on changes in quantities imported and exported; this impact must therefore be estimated in the framework of supply, demand or comparative advantage relationships.

Location Theory and Agglomeration Factors

Location theory was originally developed in Europe by various independent researchers and, later, was incorporated as an integral component of what has come to be called regional science by U.S. economists. Because of the lack of adequate analytical tools, the early contributors to the field have generally failed to build a general spatial equilibrium theory of interdependence between regions. They have, however, theorized about the process of locational choice of firms and recognized the agglomeration forces which attract industries towards established economic centers.

1. Industrial Location.   Industrial location theory is of relevance in that it gives some insight into what creates differentials between regions in a spatial general equilibrium framework.

Essentially a firm will tend to select a production site where the supply and demand conditions can be combined in a profit-maximizing formula, and a region will prosper or decline because changes in supply and demand conditions alter the attractional value of its sites. The complexity of the location problem arises from the fact that the materials required in the production process cannot often be supplied from a single region, and that price differentials exist between suppliers. Price differentials reflect, of course, the variations in resource endowment and are the quantitative expressions of comparative advantage. Once distance relationships between market and input suppliers are costed, it becomes possible to determine supply and demand curves for each location, and therefore to find the location where a firm can maximize its profits.

The theory leads to the general finding that if the factor cost differentials are relatively small the optimal location depends upon the particular characteristics of the production process used by the firm. If the process involves a substantial reduction in bulk from materials to the product, such as refining of ores, the location of the firm is necessarily oriented to the source of the material. If the process involves a substantial increase in bulk by the use of ubiquitous materials, such as manufacturing of soft drinks, it is necessarily oriented to the location of the market. If the nature of the process lies between these two extremes, the optimal location depends subtly upon other factors, such as transportation and factor cost differentials. The existence of transportation costs determine the pull that material site, labor pool, and consumer markets are exerting on a particular firm or group of firms. Depending on which predominates in the locational calculus, industries have been traditionally classified as material, labor, or market oriented.

Transportation costs, of course, depend on distances, but they are influenced to a great extent by the "transportability" characteristics of the product. While distances do not change, products and production technologies do change in a progressive economy. In the process, the equilibrium between the locational pulls of labor, materials, and market can be considerably altered. Indeed, observations made of locational changes over the past three decades have generally shown that natural resource sites have lost most of their attractional power. More will be said in the next chapter on these exogenous developments which introduce a host of limitations upon a static analysis of the interregional distribution of activities.

Locational shifts may also be induced from changes in the transportation cost structure, resulting from transportation innovation or from rate changes. At this juncture, a critical distinction must be made in the ways transportation changes occur. Such changes may lower the whole structure of transportation costs simultaneously and equally in all directions, or they may modify this structure by benefiting some users more than others. In a country depending exclusively on rail transportation, a general and a regional decrease in railroad rates illustrate both cases. To a large extent, a transportation innovation, while it reduces costs absolutely, tends also to change the entire structure. The advent of trucking has, for instance, greatly decreased the transportation costs between centers located in the same region, such as Boston and Springfield, Massachusetts, without affecting the rail advantage between centers located at greater distances, such as Boston and Chicago.

Most economists who have tried to explain recent trends in patterns of geographical shifts have given considerable locational significance to the relationship between short and long distance transportation costs. In general, a *relative* reduction of short distance transportation costs will encourage industry to move closer to its market. Since such a reduction tends to "regionalize" activities, it should, therefore, be interpreted as a decentralizing force. On the other hand, reduction of long-distance costs, resulting, for instance, from improvements in containerization or railroading will obviously tend to have the opposite effects and concentrate industries in a few selected areas, since manufacturers will be able to serve these customers from farther away.

2. **Agglomeration Factors and Location.**   Provided that costs do not vary with the level of operation, it is relatively easy to determine the location which satisfies the profit maximizing objective. A contribution of location theory has

been to discard this assumption and to show that as a result of cost declining with plant size, location decisions are much influenced by the existing geographical distribution of consumption and production centers. Similarly, agglomeration economies represent the benefits derived from locating near established centers, and explain much of the actual distribution of economic activities.

Because of the existence of agglomeration economies, the location decisions of firms and industries are interdependent; and hence the location problems are often indeterminate. As a result, neither location nor trade theories have been very successful at incorporating agglomeration factors in analytical models. Of course, the theoretical indeterminacy of the location problem has been solved in practice by historical development.

The tendency to agglomerate cannot be attributed to a single cause; it results in fact from the convergence of three sets of phenomena which location theorists have classified into scale, localization, and urbanization economies. For a firm, the three types of economies need not climax at the same point in time; in fact, they rarely do. A firm that has been originally attracted by the prospect of achieving economies of scale, but that has grown to the point where it suffers diseconomies of scale, may elect to stay in the city because it enjoys localization and urbanization economies.

Economies of scale are internal to a firm and refer to the advantage of producing in large quantities, or more technically to situations where the average cost falls when the quantity produced increases. Such economies originate from the imperfect divisibility of machinery and equipment and from a host of other similar reasons which need no elaboration here. The essential fact remains that economies of scale induce firms to concentrate their activities geographically. As one result, the dispersion effect of high transportation costs has been historically mitigated. One of the most significant trends toward concentration due to economies of scale in recent decades is the development of suburban shopping centers away from minute grocery and other convenience stores. Although scale economies have played an important role in concentrating activities, they are more difficult to observe today since most firms in the United States may be operating at a level where they are no longer marginally as significant.

Localization economies refer to the benefits accruing to firms within a single industry from locating near each other. To a large extent, the automotive industry typifies the industry subject to localization economies. On the other hand, urbanization economies refer to the benefits derived from the geographical closeness of a variety of altogether different industries. Because of the sheer size of the pooled common expenditures, these industries might enjoy, for example, better public services at cheaper rates. They may also avail themselves of a host of differentiated private services such as easy borrowing, access to research and development centers, and better business services which can be supported only by a large community. Although the two types of economies are quite different in nature, they both result from complementarity and linkages among firms. Historically, agglomeration economies tend to be self-cumulative so that development becomes bound by an irreversible historical pattern.

There is, unfortunately, no consensus on the extent and magnitude of agglomeration factors, and the studies aimed at statistically measuring geographical interdependence of industries have failed to yield conclusive evidence. It is generally admitted, however, that new trends in production technology, such as greater divisibility of equipment and of input requirements, tend to reduce the significance of large scale economies and, in fact, may justify relocation. Over and above the benefits of relocation, however, economies of localization and urbanization tend to discourage firms from moving away individually.[11]

Neoclassical Integration: Interregional Programming

Since the notion of transportation advantage is intellectually interesting as well as practically significant, modern mathematically oriented economists have attacked the problem of making it operational. As a result, a spatial general equilibrium theory has been developed and with it a tool of analysis called the interregional programming technique.[12] The purpose of these programming models is to find the best way to achieve certain results while staying within the limits of a given problem. In the field of transportation, linear programming techniques can be designed to manage a simple operation, such as a railroad yard, or an entire transport system, in attaining certain objectives. Although the principles of linear programming are simple, the mathematical structure is complex and the data requirements can be large.

The basic premise of interregional linear programming models is similar to that made by classical trade theory: a region will manufacture the goods and services which are profitable to produce and deliver at the market place, and build its specialization around the corresponding activities. At a given point in time, the capacity of a region, both as a consuming and as a production unit, sets certain constraints upon any solution to the problem. The spectrum of transportation cost relationships, as reflected in the models, expresses transportation networks as they exist and allows explicit consideration of factors such as transshipment costs and rate structure differentials. The impact of transportation programs on the interregional distribution of activities is analyzed in the models by systematic manipulations of the transportation cost variables and observation of the responses which they generate in the distribution of economic activities. Several transportation linear programming models have been conceptualized for the United States and other countries. As a rule these models[13] are designed

---

11. Raymond Vernon, *Metropolis 1985* (Cambridge: Harvard University Press, 1960.)

12. See Appendix for a description of some transportation programming models.

13. See for example, Mitchell Harwitz and Arthur P. Hurter, *Transportation and the Economy of the Appalachian Region*, Transportation Center at Northwestern University, Report No. 66, August, 1964.

determine which interregional flow of commodities gives a maximum (or minimum) value to a certain objective function, while satisfying consumption and production capacity constraints. The objective function usually consists of minimizing the costs of delivered goods. The constraints require that the flow of goods cover the demand of each region without exacting from a region more than it can produce. Such a model typically assumes: (1) a fixed production capacity in each region for each commodity; (2) a fixed demand in each region for each commodity; (3) the possibility to produce and consume all products in all regions; and (4) immobility of resources in each region. Besides the optimal interregional flow of commodities, such a model can determine the prices of all commodities and the relative production advantage (rent) for each region. It is, therefore, possible to assign priorities in development programs. The model indicates also the regional gaps between actual production and industrial capacity.

The application of linear algebra to trade theory permits a good theoretical grasp of the spatial general equilibrium relationship between regions. It is also a significant planning tool since it makes it possible to predict the impact of changes in the transportation network on the interregional activity pattern, or to implement a particular policy. It is possible to determine how a region will be affected (favorably or otherwise) by changes in transportation costs, and what kind of industries it will lose to or attract from other regions, as a result of extension of the network.

While the linear programming approach appears to be a powerful analytical tool in investigating the impact of transportation programs, its use is subject to practical limitations. To begin, the underlying assumptions are obviously quite restrictive. The models developed have rarely been tested on real or even contrived data. Furthermore, the models are static and must be revised to incorporate the effects of changes in production or transportation technology. Finally, they do not achieve a complete general interregional equilibrium where regional supplies and demands are interdependent with the transportation system.

Benefit-Cost and Capital Budgeting Techniques

From the time of Adam Smith it has been suggested that competitive behavior of optimizing individuals generally leads to an efficient resource allocation. Later economists introduced the concept of marginal analysis and gave a technical proof to the hypothesis of identity of competitive equilibrium and efficient resource allocation. Modern mathematically oriented economists have attacked the problem in fine detail. The general result of the analysis is the following: in the absence of monopolistic firms, economies of scale, and external economies, the resource allocation based on the individual profit motive leads to an efficient allocation of resources throughout the system.

The above finding is quite useful for policy formulation in many sectors of the economy, but it may not be readily applicable to the transportation sector, because many of the assumptions of the theory are violated to one degree or another. For example, one widely held notion is that market peculiarities in the transportation industry necessitate strong regulatory practices by government, in this country and elsewhere. However, as Meyer, et. al. argue in *The Economics of Competition in the Transportation Industries*,[14] transport may deviate little in competitive characteristics from other sectors in the present state of our economy. Furthermore, since we are concerned with the regional viewpoint but not with that of any single firm, most external economies can be thought of as internalized within the region.

Therefore, in the absence of monopolistic pricing through either competition or regulation, the efficiency of the regional transportation system as a whole or of any part could be tested on the basis of the normal profit condition which should prevail in every firm and sector under perfect competition. That is, the return to the investment in any transportation facility within the region should be above or equal to the opportunity cost of the investment, i.e., the return which can be expected from any other profitable investment project. If the rate of return is below the opportunity cost, the regional transportation system is overinvested. If it is abnormally high, investment must continue until the rate of return goes down to the opportunity cost due to diminishing returns. This rule at least gives a practical guide to the formulation of a regional investment policy in transportation.[15]

One can imagine, however, a case in which a region is in equilibrium and then a subsidy program is introduced for the transportation sector. Before the subsidy program, the rate of return on the marginal transport investment should equal the opportunity cost. After the initiation of the new program, the real cost of transport investments is reduced by the subsidy program. Therefore the rational strategy for the region is to increase investment in transportation until the rate of return comes down to the new, subsidized and therefore lower opportunity cost. As a result, the bundle of transportation projects within the region will be increased substantially. In the real world, however, two factors complicate the picture. First, the costs of maintenance and replacement in the future may not be subsidized in the same manner. Therefore, the subsidy program may not

---

14. John R. Meyer, Merton J. Peck, John Stenason and Charles Zwick, *The Economics of Competition in the Transportation Industries*, (Cambridge: Harvard University Press, 1959).

15. See Roland McKean, *Efficiency in Government Through Systems Analysis* (New York: Wiley and Sons, Inc., 1958); Arthur Maass, ed., *Design of Water-Resource Systems* (Cambridge: Harvard University Press, 1962); Otto Eckstein, *Water-Resource Development: The Economics of Project Evaluation* (Cambridge: Harvard University Press, 1958), especially pp. 19–46; and John V. Krutilla and Otto Eckstein, *Multiple Purpose River Development: Studies in Applied Economic Analysis* (Baltimore: Johns Hopkins University Press for Resources for the Future, 1958), especially Chapter 2, "The Concept of Efficiency."

necessarily expand services but only the "capital intensity" of projects. Second, matching funds may be required and local governments generally have limited matching funds and these often can be expanded only with considerable effort. This tends to constrain the expansion of the investment budget.

The order of magnitude of the increase in regional income induced by a transport investment can be analyzed by benefit-cost techniques. However, the benefit-cost technique is not capable of accounting for the system effects such as the effects of price changes and changes in production other than that of the project itself. Due to these secondary effects the actual gain in regional income will be different, usually larger, than the amount which the benefit-cost analysis predicts. To solve this problem quantitatively, a simulation model of the economic system which includes the region is required, as outlined in the next section.

Simulation and Other Behavioral Models

Simulation models are conceptually and practically more promising than other models for analyzing the impact of transport investments because of their comprehensiveness. They can encompass many sectors, regions, and modes of activity, and may include a large number of variables such as prices of goods, the production capacities of industries (even if non-linear), and factor costs and profits of each region.

Perhaps the most ambitious transport simulation model yet constructed for predicting the impact of alternative transportation projects in underdeveloped countries was that done by the Harvard Transport Research Program.[16] The model consists of two connected sub-models. The Economic Model based on a national input-output table provides the transport model with regional production and consumption data through time. The Transport Model assigns commodity flows to the network on the basis of certain behavioral assumptions.

The model traces how an improvement in a transportation system reduces the cost of production. If the cost of production is reduced, firms can increase profits if prices remain the same, or, contrarily, prices can fall. If profits are increased, they will be channeled to investment within the region or elsewhere. If prices are reduced, the region gains competitive advantages. Labor, materials, and distribution costs being lowered, expansion of production occurs in the region on an aggregate and per capita basis.

------

16. John R. Meyer, ed., *Techniques of Transport Planning* (Washington: The Brookings Institution, 1971), Vol. II, David Kresge and Paul O. Roberts, *System Analysis and Simulation Models*.

Empirical Appraisal of the Role of Transportation in Regional Growth: Past and Future

Summary of the Theory

So far, the regional impact of transportation has been surveyed from the viewpoint of theory, and empirical evidence has been called upon only occasionally. Briefly, the theory ultimately relates growth to regional exports but it also indicates that the economic impetus from the development of an export base depends on the intraregional integration of production and consumption activities.

Transportation becomes a critical factor in regional growth since it determines the extent to which an area can capitalize on its economic endowment for generating exports. In a general sense, the endowment of a region is determined by the cost of its labor force, the abundance of its materials, the size of its markets and the agglomeration factors of its urban centers. Because these four locational factors vary geographically, regions differ in the attractional pull that they exert on industry. Given a set of transportation costs, industries find a profitable location (spatial equilibrium) among these factors. The theory suggests that a general downward trend in transportation costs reinforces the influence of production cost differentials in the locational decision. Many changes in the transportation network also transform the cost structure (relationships between different sources and destinations) and therefore tend to change the whole pattern of industrial distribution among regions. Such effects are specific and depend on the nature and direction of shifts in the transportation cost structure; it is not possible to generalize their regional impact on *a priori* grounds.

Empirical Studies

In general, the literature that has explored the actual relationship between transportation and development is too fragmentary to provide a good test of theory. Under the auspices of the Bureau of Public Roads, a large number of highway impact studies have been conducted by universities and private organizations.[1] A primary concern of many of these studies has been to determine the locational

---

1. For a good summary of such economic studies, see *Highways and Economic and Social Changes*, U. S. Department of Commerce, Bureau of Public Roads, Washington, D.C., 1964.

effects produced in the immediate vicinity of the highway link. Because of this limited scope, no extensive analysis is done of the geographical origin of the attracted industries, a consideration of paramount importance when regional growth is under scrutiny.

A more promising approach would be to evaluate predictive models (e.g., those based on input-output or activity analysis) to determine how the results which they yield deviate from reality.[2] The accuracy of these models depends on a number of considerations, e.g., the homogeneity of commodity groups being used, the extent of geographic differences in seasonal productive patterns, etc. To the extent the models reflect the most relevant variables and are properly applied, they constitute a useful tool for transportation planning. Unfortunately, such models are still in a developmental stage and have not been widely implemented in practice.

The Historical Record

An attempt also can be made to ascribe the role of transportation from an analysis of the actual shifts in locational patterns described in the economic literature.[3] That is, an empirical appraisal of the role of transportation in regional

---

2. For a theoretical treatment of the use of input-output techniques see Wassily Leontief and Alan Strout, "Multiregional and Input-Output Analysis;" in Tibor Barna, ed. *Structural Interdependence and Economic Development*. (London: Macmillan, 1963). Harvard University Doctoral Dissertations, Mario S. Brodersohn, "A Multi-regional Analysis of the Argentine Economy" and Karen R. Polenske, "A Case Study of Transportation Models Used in Multi-regional Analysis" are useful examples of the application of input-output techniques. Koichi Mera, "Evaluation of Techniques for Assignment of Interregional Commodity Flows," Harvard Transportation and Economic Development Seminar Discussion Paper No. 22, compares the predictive accuracy of gravity and linear programming models in a particular case. Richard J. Bouchard and Clyde E. Pyers, "Use of Gravity Model for Describing Urban Travel;" in Highway Research Record No. 88, *Travel Patterns – 8 Reports* (Washington: NAS-NRC publication No. 1304, 1964) and W. G. Hansen, "Evaluation of Gravity Model Trip Distribution Procedures;" in Highway Research Board Bulletin No. 347 (Washington: Highway Research Board, 1962) offer a detailed discussion of the use of gravity models. See Mitchell Harwitz and Arthur P. Hurter, *Transportation and the Economy of the Appalachian Region*, Transportation Center at Northwestern University, Report No. 66, 1964, for a multi-regional linear programming model.

3. The major works investigated were: Simon Kuznets, Ann R. Miller and Richard A. Easterlin, *Analysis of Economic Change*, Vol. II of *Population Redistribution and Economic Growth, United States 1870-1950*, prepared under the direction of Simon Kuznets and Dorothy S. Thomas (Philadelphia: American Philosophical Society, 1960); for the period 1929-1954, Harvey S. Perloff, et al., *Regions, Resources and Economic Growth* (Baltimore: Johns Hopkins Press, 1960); and Victor Fuchs, *Changes in the Location of Manufacturing in the United States Since 1929* (New Haven: Yale University Press, 1962). Ample use is also made of the New York Metropolitan Region Study conducted by the Harvard University Graduate School of Public Administration, the results of which have been published in a number of titles. See especially Benjamin Chinitz, *Freight and the Metropolis* and Robert Lichtenberg, *One Tenth of a Nation* (both Cambridge: Harvard University Press, 1960).

growth can be made by associating the historical development of transportation with shifts in geographical distribution of activities.[4]

The Ubiquity of the Transportation Network

We shall not discuss in detail here the phenomenal expansion of the transportation network that started a century ago and the general downward trend in transportation costs that ensued. We may say, however, that this expansion proceeded in three stages corresponding successively to the introduction of the railroad, the automobile, and the airplane. From a mere 8,000 miles in 1850, the railroad network spurted to 31,000 miles in 1860, 164,000 in 1890, to an all-time high of 265,000 in 1915. The federal-aid highway system which extended over 170,000 miles in 1923, covered 911,000 miles in 1968. The route mileage of air transportation, which was non-existent in 1924, is more than 138,000 now.

The current extent of the system is summarized in Table 3-1.

Table 3-1
Miles of Transportation Right-of-Way Facilities in the United States

Mode	Mileage	Date
Railroads[a]	211,642	1969
Improved waterways[b]	25,543	1969
Rural highways[c]		
Nonsurfaced	770,401	1969
Low-type surface[d]	1,229,486	1969
Intermediate-type surface[e]	656,485	1969
High-type surface[f]	505,354	1969
Pipelines (oil)[g]	170,824	1969
Airways (federal)[h]	138,450	1969

[a]Interstate Commerce Commission, *Transport Statistics in the U.S. Year Ended December 31, 1969,* Part I, p. 3. Class I line-haul.

[b]American Waterways Operators, Inc., *Inland Water-Borne Commerce Statistics for the Calendar Year 1969.* (Washington, D.C., 1969), p. 1.

[c]Bureau of Public Roads, *Highway Statistics, 1969,* p. 183.

[d]Types D and E, under Bureau of Public Roads classification.

[e]Types F, G-1, H-1.

[f]Types G-2, H-2, I, and J.

[g]Interstate Commerce Commission, *Transport Statistics in the U.S. Year Ended December 31, 1969,* Part 6, p. 4.

[h]*Statistical Abstract of the U.S., 1970,* U.S. Dept. of Commerce, Bureau of the Census, p. 563.

4. See in particular Benjamin Chinitz, "Differential Regional Economic Growth: Impact on and of Transportation;" in National Academy of Sciences-National Research Council, *Transportation Design Considerations* (Washington: NAS-NRC publication 841, 1961).

Locational Shifts[5]

For the past hundred years, geographical shifts in industries and populations have occurred in the United States because of fundamental technological and economic changes that modify the profit or utility maximizing calculations of the important decision units, particularly households and business firms. It can hardly be overstressed that these locational shifts have not been determined exclusively by transportation considerations; changes in manufacturing and other production technologies and changes in the composition of economic activity that occur with growth or development as well as changes in patterns of consumer taste have been at least as important as transportation changes in determining shifts in industrial and population locations.

At the earliest stage of U. S. development, as in most economies, agriculture and raw material exploitation were emphasized. In essence, each region of the nation participated in the national expansion on the basis of its comparative advantage in raw material and agricultural resources. From a locational standpoint, however, the outstanding feature of agriculture and raw material extraction is that these activities need a physical location near required land and resources. Basically, the development of such activities, particularly agriculture, implies a dispersal of population over the land surface of the nation or of the region whose economy is undergoing development.

This is not to say that this dispersal is necessarily uniform. The development of commercial and transportation centers and facilities to serve agriculture and mining gave rise to a hierarchy of urban or semi-urban centers or nodes, much after the fashion described by classical location theories.

Furthermore, early manufacturing development in the United States actually prompted some additional dispersal. The primitive character or nonexistence of technologies for transmitting power in the nineteenth century, and the consequent need to rely almost totally on waterfalls for early manufacturing power, meant that manufacturers had to be located near − virtually upon − the falls or rapids of rivers. The pattern is particularly evident in New England but is also observable in most other parts of the country, even including the Far West, as for example on the Willamette River. The relatively early development of heavy industries with a strong raw material orientation, such as steel, also tended to develop further nodes that were largely dictated by transportation considerations in relation to sources of basic raw material inputs. In the jargon of location theory (see Chapter 2) these were process-oriented rather than market-oriented industries. In short, site locations for early manufacturing activities in the United States were, like those for agriculture and mining, not particularly dictated by the location of markets or any great need to be near existing urban settlements. They tended

---

5. Much of the material in this section is adapted from John R. Meyer, "Regional and Urban Locational Choices in the Context of Economic Growth," an address prepared for presentation at the University of Illinois as the D. Philip Locklin Lecture for the Academic Year 1965–66.

rather to be located near whatever raw materials, power sources, or agricultural
land was required.

A very fundamental change occurred near or just before the beginning of
this century. Our economic development shifted toward lighter industries and
service activities. As our national product has grown, its composition also has
changed from more commodities to more services. Service activities over an
eighty-year period have multiplied by twelve. For these the locational advantage
tended to be near major markets and sources of labor. A major contributing
factor was the structure of transportation rates. Under value-of-services or value-
of-commodities tariffs, finished goods tended to bear a much higher percentage
markup over cost than transport of raw materials.

At a slightly later date, these transport considerations, which favored a
market-oriented location for the newer and lighter industries, were reinforced by
the development of the internal combustion engine and truck transport; the
truck, as noted previously, tended to reduce the cost of short haul transport relatively more than of long haul transport.

The newer and lighter industries developing at or around the turn of the
century also found it advantageous to avail themselves of the externalities of
urban locations, that is, of so called urban agglomeration economies.[6] These
were particularly important as they effected the recruitment and the development
of a flexible or adaptable work force. Considerable economies of scale were also
present in the development of certain types of urban infrastructure; these ultimately could or would reflect themselves in lower cost at an urban location. This
is not to argue that such economies of scale could not or have not eventually ex-
hausted themselves in very large urban agglomerations. The point is, rather, that
given the status of urban development at the beginning of this century, reasonably
high qualities of urban facilities were more inexpensively developed in or around
our largest and medium-sized cities than by starting *de novo* new cities or by expanding sharply on the limited basis of small towns. These developments meant
that the larger commercial, transportation, and manufacturing nodes which had
developed earlier, that is during the nineteenth century for the most part, tended
to become growth points as the twentieth century began.

Relatively rapid rates of productivity improvement in agriculture, transportation, and heavy manufacturing heightened these trends. That is, the relative
importance of these activities not only declined within our economy but the man-
power requirement per unit of output also tended to decline relatively more
rapidly than for service or most light manufacturing industries.

A correlative, reinforcing, locational trend that also began somewhere near
the turn of the century is that of a "decentralization of industry". It has been
alluded to in several empirical studies.[7] The "decentralization of industry" referred to is normally defined as a trend that spreads the distribution of industries

---

6. Chinitz, *Freight*, and Perloff, et al., op. cit.

7. Chinitz, *Freight*, and Fuchs, op. cit.

more evenly throughout the country. Activities once heavily concentrated in a particular area are attracted to or appear in new areas. However, this phenomenon does not imply an increase in industrial density of the urban countryside. On the contrary, while a region enlarges the spectrum of activities in which it partici- pates, urban centers most frequently will benefit most from such changes. De- centralization and urban concentration are, therefore, quite possibly compatible.

In large measure, in fact, the decentralization of industry represents a type of import substitution that occurs on a regional or local basis in almost any economy as the size of its local markets grow in terms of both population and purchasing power. For example, as population has drifted toward the western and southwestern portions of the United States, the metropolitan centers of these regions have increasingly found themselves capable of supporting an ever-wider range of efficient manufacturing industries and services at the local level.

Decentralization is also partly explained by causes which tend to render industries more mobile, more footloose:[8] these are attributable among other things to drastic changes in production technology, to shifts in demand, and to the opening of the amenity resource frontier, as will be developed later in this chapter.

Population and industrial growth in the West and Southwest also relate to another important aspect of recent locational patterns. Specifically, resource- oriented development of new commercial centers or cities has never been totally arrested in our economy. While of far more relative importance during the nine- teenth century than thus far in the twentieth, the development of new resources, particularly petroleum, has kept in motion certain basic population dispersal tendencies in our economy and also has helped create new transportation and commercial knowledge of considerable importance. In general, there is nothing either discontinuous or sharply delineated in defining different phases of development.

Another major trend in American locational patterns has to do with popula-

---

8. The concept of "footloose" industry is subject to different interpretations. In a restricted sense, the term refers to an industry which is neither material nor labor oriented. It is evident that now this definition would apply to most industries. In a more general sense, a footloose industry is defined as an industry which shows, in addition to the above characteristics, only a weak attraction to markets. (See, for instance, the definition given by Perloff in *How a Region Grows — Area Development in the U. S. Economy*, (Committee for Economic Development — Supplementary Paper No. 17, March 1963). Although the spectrum of locational alternatives is wide for a footloose industry, such industry is not completely indifferent to choices among many site locations. The weight of locational factors are simply different from those of classical trade theory, and may be topped by climate, for instance. Obviously, only a few industries fit the above description at present. Among them, we may mention the drug industry, the electronics industry, and a large portion of nonpolitical government activities. It is our contention, however, that the number of such industries is increasing. For a footloose industry, the existence of transportation costs is not a primary consideration in the locational calculus, although the latter may be influenced by other modal attributes, such as speed and regularity of services, traffic capacity, etc.

tion and work-place distributions within our major urban areas. Specifically, advances in transportation, communications, bookkeeping, manufacturing, and retailing technologies have tended to make different parcels of land increasingly homogenous within our urban areas for most productive functions.[9]

The same is often increasingly true of residential locations. The relevant point for present purposes is that these changes have tended to make location at points of very high density within our urban areas less attractive than location at peripheral urban sites of medium to low density. A more uniform distribution of activities over the urban surface is the result. This has been achieved *both* by reducing concentration of existing points of maximum density, that is, so-called central business districts, and increasing densities of less central sites within our urban areas. Thus, if we were to plot density of population of activities around the vertical axis of a two-dimension diagram, and distances from central business district along the horizontal and to the right, we would increasingly find that the functional relationship between these two variables is becoming less steeply inclined, dropping on the left and rising on the right.

The net effect of these different locational forces operating in the context of a modern economy or technology is not too difficult to discern. On the one hand, they suggest the development of a society that is increasingly urban. On the other, the maximum point density of population and of work places within these urban areas is declining; work activity and population densities in urban areas are becoming essentially uniform, or at least more uniform. In short, we see two fundamental locational trends at work. One, so to speak, has pushed population toward our larger urban agglomerations and the other is pushing downward on the maximum point densities of population of work places within these agglomerations. Again, changes in transport technology, which are often singled out as the prime or only cause of locational changes, while still important, are not the only forces operative in shaping today's locational patterns. Basic trends in the mix of industrial and economic activities and changes in productive technologies employed in producing goods and services within our society are at least as important as transport as determinants of choices.

As compared to fifty years ago, the production process also has become highly divisible and the number of steps between materials and the finished product has increased. Where products used to be processed from beginning to finish in the same area, plants are now assembling parts shipped from several distant locations. The computer industry, which requires a multitude of small, elaborate components, offers a good example of this new trend. An obvious result is again a lessening of the attractional pull exercised by raw material sites; to a large extent, the locational decision is influenced by the location of the suppliers and buyers who are not the ultimate consumers but who are other producers further

---

9. For documentation of these trends, see J. Meyer, J. Kain and M. Wohl, *The Urban Transportation Problem* (Cambridge: Harvard University Press, 1965), Chapters 2 and 3.

along the production chain. While it is true that the locations of different producers along this chain are theoretically interrelated, whether this interdependence generates actual geographical linkages is by no means evident. The fact that, at each stage of production, a variety of components coming from various geographical origins and even from different industries (wood, steel, plastic, etc.) is assembled tends to open a vast panorama of site alternatives.

In the past decades, technical skills also have become more ubiquitous and education has been spreading more evenly throughout the country. While differentials still exist, the educational gap is being reduced, and seems also to have a lesser locational impact. Once more, the electronics industry provides a good illustration. In its early stage, the industry developed around the nation's best laboratories and universities. Gradually, however, standardized skills, available almost everywhere, replaced scientific skills on the production line, and the industry started to decentralize, as witnessed by the opening of IBM plants in Boulder, Colorado and Lexington, Kentucky. Obviously such sites have not been selected at random: both are university locations. The fact remains that state university engineers have broken into what was once the monopoly of M.I.T. or Caltech engineers.[10] Again, this contributes to industrial decentralization and reduced dependence of industry on raw material or resource sites.

Decentralization and Transportation

Transportation: A Direct Cause of Decentralization

As noted, economists have explained the dispersion of industrial activities (or the increase in regional self-sufficiency, which amounts to the same thing) at least partially on the basis of technological differences between modes.[11] The central point of their discussion revolves around the ratio of short haul to long haul costs. A decline in short haul costs *relative* to long haul costs tends to disperse activities by promoting industrialization around regional markets, whereas an opposite shift in the ratio stimulates the reverse trend. One result, accordingly, often attributed to highway programs and to the development of truck transportation is to modify the transportation structure in favor of short haul movements of goods. This relative improvement of truck transportation over rail, helps explain why the local producer can now successfully compete with the distant large-scale producer,

10. Daniel Shimshoni, "Regional Development and Science-Based Industry," in *Essays in Regional Economics,* John F. Kain and John R. Meyer, eds. (Cambridge: Harvard University Press, 1971.)

11. The discussion which follows has been extensively developed by Chinitz. In addition to the work by this author already cited, see Benjamin Chinitz and Raymond Vernon, "Changing Forces in Industrial Location," *Harvard Business Review,* January–February, 1960. The argument is basically an empirical interpretation of Hoover's location theory. For this see Edgar M. Hoover, *The Location of Economic Activity* (New York: McGraw-Hill, 1948), Chapter 10.

simply by compensating for higher costs of production by somewhat lowered delivery costs.

The advantage of truck over rail on short distances needs a little elaboration. The existence of a cost differential between the two modes rests on a fairly important distinction between two kinds of costs incurred in the transportation of commodities: the line haul costs and the terminal costs. Line haul costs are those involved with the physical movement of freight between two locations; they are, therefore, roughly proportional to distance. Terminal costs are incurred in loading and delivering the freight at the points of origin and destination; their magnitude depends, among other things, on the flexibility of the system itself; usually they do not fluctuate with distances. Because of the relative ubiquity of the highway network, it is not surprising that the terminal costs are smaller, as indicated by cost studies, for truck transportation. On short distances at least, the cost of the entire trip is minimized with truck rather than rail transportation. Consequently, producers could increasingly locate nearer their markets, which results in a "regionalization" of industry, without loss as truck technology developed. Other advantages of truck transportation for short distances (greater speed, decline in the cost of shipping smaller lots as compared to large lots) have also contributed to the dispersion of industries previously concentrated in few areas.

New developments in transportation technology might generate powerful forces which could counterbalance the decentralization effects of trucking. One is the anticipated cut in long haul air cargo rates resulting from the technological and economical feasibility of giant cargo planes. Another, the piggyback technique or containerization, combines the low terminal cost of truck transportation with the low long-haul cost of rail transportation and promises substantial decreases in costs of intermediate length hauls. In theory, both innovations extend the market of large, distant producers and adversely affect the position of local plants, thus reinforcing the concentration of activities in specific regions. The full impact of these new developments depends, obviously, on the rate structure and regulations which will be imposed on them. Furthermore, as pointed out in the last section, it must be remembered that transport is only one of many factors conditioning locational choices.

In general, we should not bind our analysis by a transportation-based determinism. On that basis, we would conclude that technological trends would recentralize activities and impair the chances of the slow-growing regions to attract industry. However, this ignores the fact that the true decentralizing forces generally have originated outside the transportation field.

Transportation: An Indirect Cause of Decentralization

As noted, new developments in production technology, product characteristics and demand have reduced the importance of transportation costs in the locational calculus and increased the mobility of industries by dissociating them from the traditional poles of locational attraction. Modal characteristics other than costs may, however, play an important role in the attraction of footloose industries to a particular location.

As the production process expands into new phases, the production of high value, lightweight products tends to increase. The product value comes to represent more labor (e.g., engineering skill and scientific know-how) and less material. By reducing weight and volume and increasing labor contents, the "miniaturization" of the product decreases transportation costs not only absolutely but also relative to other processing costs. This trend, coupled with the growth of the service sector, promotes the usefulness of speed, dependability, and ubiquity over low costs as the essential or desirable modal characteristics of a transportation network. It appears also that the increase in the demand for transportation of people tends to outpace that for commodities. From the observation of freight movement between 1929 and 1956, it can be argued that commodity traffic is declining in the sense that it has grown at a lower rate than output.[12] The prospect of ever increasing passenger traffic may favor the regions which provide transportation systems where flows of people both within and outside the region are rapid and easy.

As passenger transportation has improved, amenity resources have emerged among the elements that constitute the resource base of a region. In the early 1950s, social geographers had speculated that environment was, indeed, a primary determinant of regional growth and migration.[13] This hypothesis was corroborated by most studies that have analyzed locational shifts in industry. The Pacific Coast and the Southwest, two amenity-rich regions, have, in fact, been the national leaders in growth. Some empirical studies conclude that climate has become a major locational factor.[14]

A debate has opened around the direction of the relationship between transportation and "regionalization" of industry. Some economists contend that there is little left for transportation in shaping regions.[15] They maintain that, instead of directing the geography of growth, transportation will have to be adapted to the geography and growth patterns. In this sense, transportation is a result rather

---

12. On this point see Holland Hunter, "Resources, Transportation and Economic Development," in Joseph Spengler Jr., ed. *Natural Resources and Economic Growth* (Washington: Resources for the Future, 1961); and Alexander Morton, "Demands for Intercity Freight Transportation," Ph.D. thesis in process, Harvard University.

13. See Edward Ullman, "Amenities as a Factor in Regional Growth," *Geographical Review*, Vol. 44 (1954), pp. 119–132.

14. Fuchs, op. cit., pp. 26–28. The same conclusion also appears in Regional and Urban Planning Implementation, Inc., "Area Welfare – Eligibility for Development Assistance" (Cambridge, 1965, unpublished report submitted to the U.S. Department of Commerce, Area Redevelopment Administration). The latter report has been summarized in Gerald Kraft, Alan R. Willens, John B. Kaler and John R. Meyer, "On the Definition of a Depressed Area," in John F. Kain and John R. Meyer, *Essays in Regional Economics* (Harvard University Press, 1971).

15. Chinitz, "Differential Regional Economic Growth."

than a cause of economic change and policy makers should implement transportation programs on the basis of the effects of the economy on transportation rather than on the reverse since, as the theory goes, the demand for transportation is a derived demand. Other economists argue, however, that whether transportation change has caused or resulted from the mobility of industries, it has locational effects and can generate its own demand. In other words, wherever it may start, there is a chain of reactions between transportation and development.[16]

Of course, the inability of transport improvements to account for current locational trends in advanced industrialized countries may partly be explained by the phenomenal extension of the transportation network itself. Any addition is now insignificant to the whole system and has little effect in shaping regional specialization.

The fact that, to a large degree, the role of transportation in shaping regional specialization has diminished must be attributed more generally to the unleashing of powerful other forces which tend to disperse activities and increase industrial mobility. It is in the context of these forces that the future role of transportation must be evaluated.

In general, the existence of good connections with the national network is one of the important elements that entices an industry to locate in a specific region. It is, however, not the only factor and no miracle should be expected from the stimulus it can provide. For example, we have noted the increasing importance of human skills in the product of today, and, therefore, of good educational facilities in the regional environment. To a large extent, the growth-seeking areas will have to provide the various facilities traditionally monopolized by cities. This involves not only cheap power, but also good banking, good trade and exchange services, and also the amenities associated with cultural life. Obviously, developments in communication technology may reduce the need for the physical existence of such services at the local level. Furthermore, pleasant climate and scenery, the privileged resource of stranded areas, may trade-off, to some extent, with urban amenities.

Regionalization of Industry

We have seen that decentralization trends could be explained to a limited extent by the substitution of truck for rail transportation, or more generally, by a relative decline of the short-haul costs. Such development tends to favor the local producer over the long-distance producer and provokes a "regionalization" of industry around local markets. In contrast with footloose industries that cater

---

16. Harold Wein, "Transportation and Regional Change;" and Louis Lefeber, "On the Interaction of Transportation and Regional Development;" both in National Academy of Sciences-National Research Council, *Transportation Design Considerations* (Washington: NAS-NRC publication 841, 1961).

to a national market, the industries that respond to a shift in the short-haul vs. long-haul cost ratio are primarily market-oriented and may not represent a large segment of the national economy. By various estimates, such industries employ approximately 15 percent of the active U.S. population.[17] Whatever the proportion may be, the existence of transportation differentials will provoke an "ebb and flow" movement between centralization and decentralization. Whether the long-term trend is toward the ebb or the flow is a matter that can be solved only when the direction of transportation improvement is known. The development of transportation facilities between regions generates at least three kinds of differentials.

First, better intraregional transportation will result in easier and cheaper distribution as well as a closer integration of regional markets. On this account, it may attract industries producing for final consumers and activities that are technologically linked to the regional industries. The regional impact of improvement in interregional links cannot be evaluated, however, without giving consideration to national transportation programs. The impossibility of simultaneously developing the whole network results in the assignment of priority programs tending, at least temporarily, to favor certain areas. While better connections with national markets will reinforce the comparative advantage of an area, they may also divert industries from other regions by offsetting production disadvantage by a transportation advantage. Such effects are temporary and depend on the transportation strategy of other regions.

Second, the key to the role of technological innovation in regional development lies mainly in its effect on the short-haul vs. long-haul cost relationship. As we have seen, the spread of containerization and the technical feasibility of large cargo planes may tend to concentrate industry by substantially reducing the cost of long and intermediate hauls. Whether these developments will reverse the decentralization trend or simply delay it depends on the absence of countervailing forces, such as artificial rates, or the size of the transportation market that the new technology will command. After all, air transportation still represents an infinitesimal fraction of the total intercity rail and truck freight movement.

Third, discriminatory practices in the past have hindered as well as helped the development of regions. Transportation rates, in the sense that they differ according to types of commodities or directions, have locational effects on industry. Traditionally, rail has favored bulk commodities, which were charged at rates near long-run marginal costs, and has discriminated against finished products which were charged at value-of-service rates. A rate revision tending to price all services and commodities as a function of marginal cost would considerably decrease long-haul transportation rates on most manufactured commodities and could retard regionalization of industry.

---

17. See Fuchs, op cit., p. 152, and also Robert M. Lichtenberg, *One Tenth of a Nation* (Cambridge: Harvard University Press, 1960), Appendix B.

Conclusion

On the whole, transport will not greatly influence the shape of future regional development in the United States, although under certain circumstances it may help a region to capture a fair share of decentralizing industry. In this respect, service considerations more than costs may determine the attractiveness of a particular transportation network.

The diminishing role of transportation in influencing location choices should not be too surprising in a country where the network is very extensive already. Instances of geographical isolation have existed within the U.S. economy (Appalachia, Four Corners Region), and may have caused economic retardation of certain areas because of high transportation costs. It would be dangerous, however, to conclude that the construction of access routes to these areas would, by itself, redress the situation.

4

The Roles of the Various Modes in Regional Economic Development

In the preceding chapters the emphasis was on transportation in general — ton miles at some cost. This chapter will differ in focusing successively on each of the different modes. The goal is to list the effects each mode can have on development within the context of the contemporary U.S. economy.

Mode Characteristics

Any transportation mode can be described in terms of three essential engineering elements: vehicle, right-of-way, and terminal facilities. These elements are the major determinants of a mode's economic characteristics and hence of its function and advantages, in general or for certain types of transportation.[1]

The major economic characteristics of each mode are cost, speed, capacity, divisibility of capacity, safety, dependability and, when passenger transportation is considered, privacy and comfort. In modeling transportation systems, economists have focused primarily on cost, which is the most easily quantifiable variable. To some extent all economic characteristics, other than costs, also can be expressed in money terms.

Cost is certainly an important modal characteristic, but it is not always the most significant one. Speed, in particular, seems to be increasingly important, not only because of an increased demand for it, but also in terms of the autonomous effects it may induce. This is self-evident in the case of perishable commodities, where an increase in speed can widen the market in just the same way as a decrease in transportation costs does for other commodities. As the value of products increases, and transport rates fall, speed may also become relatively more important for a range of non-perishable commodities. Similarly, in passenger transport, privacy, comfort, and speed are now more important than costs in many cases, and will be weighted more heavily as incomes increase. In general, the characteristics of the modes determine their relative value in satisfying the various sorts of transportation demands.

General Effects of Cost on Location

For orientation, consider again the crude and simple model presented earlier which describes how the costs of transportation influence the general pattern of

---

1. For a treatment of modal charcteristics, functions and costs, see Meyer, Peck, Stenason and Zwich, *op. cit.* and Meyer, Kresge, and Roberts, *op. cit.,* vol. I.

industrial location. Suppose firms are affected by two forces in making locational decisions: the pull of their markets, which tends to produce decentralization and the pull of resources, which tends to produce centralization. Short-haul transportation costs act as a friction on the pull of the market, and the long-haul transportation costs act similarly with respect to the pull of resources. It is clear from this model that as long-haul costs decrease, there will be a trend towards centralization, all else unchanged, and conversely for a fall in short-haul transportation costs.

However, the "all else unchanged" assumption made in the model is dubious within the current context of the U.S. economy. Several large regional centers of population have emerged during the past half century, and others seem to be growing. The growth of these large markets alone is a powerful force towards decentralization. The pull of resources is also declining. Inputs tend to be manufactured or semi-manufactured goods which must be drawn from many sources. In such cases, the costs of bringing inputs to the firm may be almost the same, no matter which location is chosen. Further, it is not absolute costs that matter, but relative costs, and a decrease in long-haul costs (piggyback, air) could be offset by decreases in short haul cost (more highways, better engines). Finally, as was mentioned above, costs are not the only relevant aspect of transportation.

Highways

Highway transportation functions in the first instance as a highly ubiquitous collection and distribution system. The highway system of the United States is well developed, and where highways are non-existent or inadequate, geography generally presents no great problems to new construction. Further, highways can obviously accomodate a large number of vehicles with many different origins and destinations. These two characteristics combine with the mobility and relatively small capacity of motor vehicles to make the highway system ideal for door-to-door or dock-to-dock transportation.

Highway transportation as an economic resource, however, is used for short and medium distances. Truck line-haul costs are generally higher than those of either rail or water, but truck terminal costs are lower. The lower terminal costs give truck an advantage over other modes for line-hauls of less than about 200 to 250 miles.[2] Beyond that distance, higher line-haul costs offset the initial advantage of lower terminal costs. The actual range for which truck rates are less than those of other modes is currently considerably more than 200 miles, apparently because of regulatory policies. But the line-haul distance for which truck is the least-cost mode is still relatively short.

2. Gayton E. Germane, Nicholas A. Glaskowsky, and J. L. Heskett, *Highway Transportation Management* (New York: McGraw-Hill, 1963).

The highway system is also not equally well adapted for carrying all types of traffic. It is clearly well suited for passenger transport for short distances. The value of the commodity is the prime determinant of the truck's freight carrying role. The small capacity, limited power, and high average costs make trucking generally uneconomical for low-cost bulk commodities. For manufactured and semi-manufactured goods with higher value-to-weight ratios, the disadvantages of trucks are relatively unimportant and the speed advantage of highway transport makes it an economical alternative to rails. Indeed, very high value products are more likely to go by air freight than by either road or rail.

The regional impact of highways can be broken down into three parts: first, the impact of the existence of a regional distribution system on the shape of the nation's economy; second, the effects of linking subregions with regional centers and creating links internal to subregions; and finally, the role of transportation within urban centers.

This classification of the problem is also convenient for organizing industrial location trends in the economy. The role of transportation as a regional collection and distribution system is related to the trend towards regionalization of industry. Subregional systems relate to the "fallout" of activity attracted to the regional centers. And the role of urban transportation relates to the deconcentration of industry within urban centers or, in less general terms, the movement of industry to the suburbs.

The general impact of the highway system on the location of industry works on market-oriented industries through decreasing short-haul transportation costs. The availability of cheap highway transportation is a major cause of decentralization of production in many product lines. This implies that a region with the other prerequisites, such as a large market, skilled labor, etc., but an inadequate highway system, could attract industry by building highways. This argument, while true enough, probably does not fit any region in the United States, because the highway system is already well extended. Some marginal attraction for more regional industry should be created, though, whenever short-haul costs are reduced relative to long-haul costs by highway improvements.

There is, however, another way to look at the role of highways in decentralization. Industry in the United States currently has an increasing opportunity to decentralize, and incentives to do so exist that are unrelated to transportation. The decreasing degree of resource orientation, and the increasing pull of large regional markets are two outstanding causes of this trend. Decentralization is therefore likely to continue independently of any events which do or do not take place in the transportation sector, and the increasing degree of decentralization will place higher demands on the highway system. From this point of view, regions regions may need additional highway capacity to keep abreast of trends in the economy. In the same vein, better highways may help attract industry to smaller towns and cities, particularly those not to distant from major markets.

Any transportation linking the various parts of a subregion, or area, serve

essentially to integrate the economy of that area; and links between an area and
the rest of the region serve to integrate the area into the economy of the region.
The general process of integration implies several specific economic events.

Population movements, first of all, would be expected. These would be of
two sorts: from the area under consideration to the urban centers of the region,
and from the rural parts of the area to whatever urban centers exist within the
area. Of course, as development continues, there might well be a net migration
into the area. The population of an area, however, should be roughly proportional to its industry or resources, and insofar as an area is underdeveloped because its population is in this sense too large, emigration would be expected.

The area being "integrated" should also experience an increase in demand
for its products and services. This is particularly evident in the case of travel
associated services such as hotels and restaurants. But it would also tend to be
true for any other resource or products the region might have. Easy access to
regional population centers might, for example, promote agricultural production.
Access might also serve to increase the terminal facilities needed in the area, and
a wider market could induce a distributor to open agencies within the area. The
existence of products in the area might also stimulate investment. TV repair
shops, for example, are found only where TV sets are owned.

The important thing to notice about all of these "effects" is that they do
not presume that genesis of the area's growth lies within the area. The implicit assumption is that various centers quite close to the area are growing. Transportation acts to encourage a "spill-over" or "growth fallout", from the developing
centers to the presumably underdeveloped area. Growth fallout is the effect that
integrating an area into a growing regional economy should be designed to produce.

Generally, highways will do more to promote regional integration than the
other modes. Integration is not necessarily the best solution to the problem of
development, and the degree that highways integrate a region is an empirical
question which has not yet been satisfactorily answered. But given that integration is the goal, and to the extent that any transportation investment can promote this goal, highways are probably the best mode.

There is a second range of effects that highways might have for inaccessible
and underdeveloped areas that is difficult even to describe, let alone quantify. For
want of a better word, these might be called "sociological effects," although they
certainly have economic implications. Highways function to some extent as a
communications device. In this role, they may serve to disseminate ideas, desires,
and knowledge.

A state of the art on this topic hardly exists, at least within the body of
economic doctrine on regional development. The sociological effects of transportation have either been largely ignored, or noticed only in passing. This report
can, therefore, primarily offer only the observation that the sociological effects
of highways may potentially be important.

Railroads

Railroads are best suited for long-haul transportation and are particularly well suited for carrying bulk commodities. The low rolling friction of the rail and the high power of the diesel engine allow railroads to carry a large volume of traffic at low ton-mile costs. These characteristics make railroads the best mode for carrying dry bulk commodities in cases where water transportation is not an alternative.

The railroads' role in carrying manufactured commodities is limited by high terminal cost, large capacity, and low speed. The line haul costs of rail transport are lower than those of trucking, but rail terminal costs are much higher. So over short-to-medium distances, truck costs are lower than rail cost, but over long distances rail's low line haul costs make up for this initial disadvantage. Similarly, for short hauls trucking is considerably faster than rail transport, but for long hauls the railroads can become competitive in terms of speed. The large capacity of the freight car limits rail in that it increases inventory costs for the small shipper. These characteristics of rail limit its ability to carry finished goods, but they definitely do not exclude rail from the market. For long hauls rail is competitive with truck in carrying many manufactures, although, like truck, it is at a disadvantage in carrying the very high value commodities that now go by air freight.

The railroads function primarily as an interregional system. As an interregional system, the U.S. railroads are very well developed but are not as ubiquitous as highways. That is, railroads often require an additional transport system for collection and distribution, almost always a highway system. From this point of view, containerization can be considered as an extension of the railroad's degree of ubiquity, although the requirement of an auxiliary or feeder highway system remains.

The general impact that rail will have on the pattern of activity in the coming years depends heavily on rate policies, technological innovations and industrial trends.

There are several reasons for thinking that long-haul rail costs will fall over the next few years and hence that the current trend toward regional industry may be arrested. Perhaps the most dramatic reason, and the only one which has already substantially decreased rail costs, is the spreading use of containers — the trailer-on-flat car or piggyback. The use of piggyback has allowed railroads to combine some of the best features of truck transportation with low rail line-haul costs. In particular, piggyback decreases rail terminal costs (although piggyback terminal costs are higher than truck terminal costs) and decreases the railroads' disadvantage in pick-up and delivery service. The railroads are also considering a number of other technological innovations, and using some of them. Data processing systems are being increasingly used, and several fully or semi-automated yards exist. The final regional impact of these innovations is unclear, but they potentially offer considerable cost savings and improvements in service.

Rate making policy is the second area of potential change. Railroad rates
have largely been set according to the "value of commodity" principle. Freight
is divided into different, more or less homogeneous, classes, and rates are set in
relation to the average value per ton of the commodities in each class. The use of
this principle has resulted in rates on finished goods which are considerably
higher than the costs of carrying them. If average or marginal cost pricing was
used, rates on these commodities would in general fall, and the railroads would
become more competitive in the market for transporting manufactures. On the
other hand, rates on bulk commodities could increase, hence increasing the
attraction of locations closer to resources.

These trends, if they materialize, may reverse or mitigate the current trend
toward decentralization. However, the qualifications made above regarding the
increasing pull of markets and the decreasing pull of resources again apply.
It is therefore impossible to say with great assurance that a trend toward centralization on balance will or will not appear, although the consensus is that it will
not.

Railroads certainly can have an impact on regional development beyond encouraging or retarding general locational trends in the economy. But in thinking
about the more specific impacts of railroads it is necessary to distinguish between
the role of railroads in servicing an existing industrial structure and their role in
creating or spreading growth. The railroads were beyond any doubt highly
influential in developing the various regions of the United States, and there
is little doubt that a region with poor rail access has a competitive disadvantage.
There is, however, no evidence which shows that any of the regions of the United
States do lack adequate rail service. It could be argued that rail service is poor in
some areas, but this seems generally due to a lack of demand rather than to a lack
of capacity. It is doubtful, therefore, that there is much leverage left in rail transportation as a tool for regional development.

It is possible that rail service might help some areas of less than regional size.
For an area with good natural resources, particularly mineral resources, but with
no rail, or inadequate rail service, constructing a line to the area or improving the
service might be helpful. With the possible exception of Alaska, there is probably
no such area in the United States today, however. In general, then, while railroads
are, and will be in the forseeable future, vitally important to the operation of the
economy, they do not seem to have a significant role to play in regional development.

Air Transportation

Extensive air transportation is such a new phenomenon, and technological
progress in aircraft design so rapid, that it is difficult and hazardous to predict

what role air will or can play in regional development. It is possible that air transportation will eventually change the shape of the economy as much as rail and highways have done in the past.

Air transportation cannot be neatly pegged as oriented to either long or short haul. The larger and faster aircraft are economical only over long distances, but there are many types of aircraft available which can operate relatively efficiently over distances as short as 150 miles. There are two characteristics, however, which all aircraft have in common. First, for distances of more than 150–300 miles they are the fastest mode available, and, second, for any distance, they are the most expensive. These two characteristics lead air to specialization in the transportation of passengers and high value commodities where speed is important but costs are not.

Certain types of aircraft also have a good deal in common with the truck. They can carry only relatively small loads from 3 to about 30 tons, and they are in a sense relatively ubiquitous, as they can land and take off on very primitive strips. This class of aircraft, generally referred to as STOL (short take-off and landing) has been of some importance in northern Canada, Alaska, the smaller Caribbean Islands, and some underdeveloped countries.

Air Passenger Transportation

Air passenger transportation can be considered in two parts: interregional and intraregional. This division is not completely satisfactory because intraregional air links largely function as feeders for the interregional trunks. But with this qualification in mind, the distinction can be useful.

A growing number of industries in the United States depend heavily on air travel. Industries with widely scattered or remote activities, such as oil drilling and some types of mining, will be oriented to general aviation. That is, these firms will tend to own and operate their own planes. R & D firms, along with the management and control portions of most large businesses, are much more likely to rely on commercial air travel. The factors which enter into the locational decisions of these activities have not been studied in detail. R & D firms in particular, are clearly not oriented to either physical inputs or to a market, since their customers are geographically scattered. Management and control activity and large service industries are oriented to urban centers and perhaps to air passenger transportation. R & D firms may, in addition, seek locations by major educational centers.

Air travel may promote a particular type of centralization in these industries. If some means of rapid travel were not available, firms would tend to open branches in the medium-sized metropolitan areas, or smaller, regionally oriented firms would emerge. The existence of air travel promotes a centralization of individual firms which sell on a national market. Centralization in this case, however, does not mean that the industry is centralized at one location, but rather that individual firms centralize in order to serve a national market.

The degree to which air travel can attract tertiary activity to a region is not clear. It is reasonable to suppose, however, that an inadequate air passenger system would decrease the attractiveness of an otherwise acceptable area. The emphasis here must be on the air passenger *system*. This means not only links to other regions, but also adequate intraregional feeder lines and adequate transportation to the airport from points within urban areas.

Air passenger transportation for strictly intraregional travel is unlikely to have any considerable effect on regional development. Building airports in underdeveloped areas, or improving existing ones, would increase access to the area. This might serve to advertise the area's advantages, and would make it more attractive as a potential site for industry. The likelihood and importance of this possibility will vary widely from area to area, but for most areas and most commodities local air travel is probably relatively unimportant.

Air Freight

The prime impact of the current and future use of jet freighters will be on the costs of long haul freight transportation. Air freight will probably not become absolutely less expensive than rail or highway for many years, but it definitely is becoming less expensive. It has been estimated, for example, that the C-5A will be very nearly competitive with transcontinental trucking. The impact of air freight will be felt long before rates become fully competitive, however, because of the advantage that air has in speed. For some commodities, e.g., cut flowers, speed in itself is necessary. In other cases, the existence of a very fast delivery system can cut the costs of doing business. A firm can cut down on inventories, for example, if it can be guaranteed rapid delivery.

Falling long-haul air freight rates could have much the same effect as declining rail rates. That is, they could tend to create industrial centralization. Paradoxically, however, the speed of air travel can also work to promote decentralization of some commodity lines. Local conditions (low wages, for example) sometimes make it desirable to "farm out" various parts of a production process. This sort of decentralization obviously requires some sort of transportation linkage between the final assembly location and the various sub-assembly production points. For commodities of relatively low value, or considerable bulk, or commodities for which assembly time is not important, rail or highway will do. But for high value products where speed is important, an air freight capability may be necessary for decentralization to occur.

The final equilibrium of these two trends is impossible to predict. The technological trend toward larger and faster jet freighters suggests that air freight will be important in interregional trade. The most striking effects of air have certainly been of interregional scope. California vegetable growers, for example, have found that air freight has opened up new markets for them on the East Coast.[3] The extent to which air freight will eventually promote specialization is uncertain, but at least in the next ten to fifteen years, its impact in this respect should be moderate. Very little freight currently moves by air, and the potential impact of air freight depends fundamentally on innovations which will substantially reduce air rates.

Other Modes

Waterways

Water transportation has relatively high terminal costs and the lowest line haul costs of all the modes except pipeline. These factors alone largely place water transportation in the long-haul market. Further, water transportation, even more than rail, is best suited for bulk commodities. The unique characteristic of both ships and barges is a tremendous capacity moved by a single power plant. This does not mean that these vessels cannot carry regular freight economically in some cases. But their greatest advantage lies in handling a large volume of bulk commodities over long hauls.

Water transportation systems have certain obvious limitations. The first is the relatively fixed nature of the channel. Waterways can, of course, be created in some cases. But this is usually a very expensive undertaking which can be justified only if a high volume of traffic is expected to persist for a fairly long period. The second limitation is equally obvious, but sometimes neglected. A water transportation system requires an ancillary system for collection and distribution. Dredging a river, for example, might make it a very desirable means of low cost transportation, but if the goods to be transported do not originate or terminate along the channel, and if transportation to or from the channel is inadequate or expensive, the improvement of the river is of little use.

The relevance of a port to the development of a region clearly depends on the existence of a port. Most regions in the United States do have ports, of course, and these are undoubtedly important. In the case of ports on inland waterways, some regions may have a substantial cost advantage because the waterways can serve to reduce the length of the more expensive land journey. Traffic on the Tennessee River, for example, has increased in part because firms located on the

---

3. Marshall D. Kochman, "New Markets for Agricultural Shippers: Problems and Opportunities," *Air Transportation*, Vol. 48, No. 5 (mid-May, 1966).

river to take advantage of savings offered by water transportation.[4] Similarly, public investment in Ohio River improvements has contributed to an industrial development in a region embracing much of a chronically depressed Appalachia.[5]

Pipelines

Pipelines are currently such a specialized mode that little need be said about their impact on development. Their major use is, and has been, in transporting petroleum, natural gas, and water over relatively long distances. As bulk carriers of these commodities, they are very efficient, and for large volumes generally the least cost mode. In the immediate future they are important only to areas which have large petroleum or gas resources.

Pipelines may play a somewhat larger role in the more distant future. In recent years, research and development in pipelines has tackled the problem of transporting solids in suspension through pipelines. At present, pipeline transportation of solids, while possible in some cases, is generally not economical. If the technical and economic problems of solid pipeline transmission are overcome, the major impact will be to decrease even further the dependency of industry on resource location and rail linkages.

---

4. J. Porter Taylor, M. I. Foster, Joseph H. McCann and Willis H. Crosswhite, *Economic Impact of Navigable Waterways* (31st International Navigation Congress, Stockholm, 1965), pp. 15–18.

5. Joseph R. Hartley, *The Economic Effects of Ohio River Navigation* (Bloomington: Indiana University Press, 1959), pp. 25–27.

5 Technological Changes and Modal Promotion Policies

Planning transportation for regional development can be regarded as the process of selecting the mode or modes to be implemented. At any point in time, the alternatives available for immediate implementation are the existing modes with their current characteristics. However, the choice among modes should be conditioned by foreseeable technological developments. Given the rapid pace of technological advance, a failure to consider new potentialities and trends could easily lead to systems which are obsolete before they are finished and hence largely a waste of resources.

A complete analysis of the impact of technological change on regional development would involve three steps. First, a description of the changes in the engineering characteristics of both existing and emerging modes, such as V/STOL and hovercraft. Second, an analysis of the influence changes in technology may have on economic characteristics such as rates and speeds over various ranges, capacity, safety and demand. And finally, a study of how changes in the transport-related economic variables in conjunction with other trends in the economy will affect regional growth.

An appropriate treatment of these aspects cannot be carried out in the short space available. This chapter, therefore, is primarily a summary of technological changes currently underway. The major goal is to indicate the innovations which planners should consider, and only secondarily to discuss the possible impact of these changes on regional development.

Air Transportation

Aircraft development is proceeding towards both slower and smaller, and faster and larger, planes. At one end of the spectrum, lower speeds and smaller vehicles increase the door-to-door capability of air travel and the capacity of major airports. A high capacity, low speed "air bus," for example, may be designed to operate over relatively short hauls either within regions or between adjacent regions along dense corridors. At a slightly higher range of speed, large subsonic jets promise lower costs for long haul domestic and international passenger and freight movements. Finally, the supersonic transports may, for long hauls, approximate the present day costs of subsonic jets, although SST costs will probably be higher than those of large subsonic jets currently being used or under development.

47

Air technology is not evolving uniformly over these speed and capacity ranges. V/STOL development lagged for some time, but defense sources have now given strong backing to their design. The V/STOL aircraft, however, still have much development ahead of them. Considerable resources are being devoted to the development of large jet freighters, air buses and, of course, SST's. Automated landing and take-off, automated airway and airport all-weather operations may be lagging behind the potentialities of electronics and behind the capabilities of large subsonic jets and SST's.

Vertical- and Short-Take-off-and-Landing (VTOL-STOL) Aircraft

V/STOL aircraft are becoming economical because of the potentialities of the gas turbine. An internal combustion engine can provide only about 1 h.p. per pound of weight, while a gas turbine can provide 5 to 8. The jet engine operating in a vertical direction, on the other hand, is very inefficient compared to the helicopter powered by an internal combustion engine. Development, therefore, has been directed toward highly augmented lift flaps or a deflection of the jet itself to give increased lift for take-off, and such aerodynamic measures as boundary layer control combined with high-lift flap and slot arrangements.

Solution of the V/STOL's engineering problems will considerably reduce the time required for trips under 200 miles, effectively giving passengers[1] in almost any part of a region ready access to major air trunk lines. An 80-passenger VTOL aircraft cruising between 200 and 400 knots for a 50 to 200 mile distance is a possible development by 1975-1980. Shorter range VTOL aircraft could be very useful in moving people within a metropolitan region to a central airport. A region might, for example, have one trunk airport and several VTOL landing pads distributed about the city. STOL aircraft can now land at between 60 to 70 knots, and so require about a 1,500 foot runway. Such planes could use 95 percent of existing U.S. airfields. Indeed, STOL aircraft have found a primary application in inaccessible or sparsely settled regions. They might, however, have some additional use in the United States as feeders on very low density routes or in place of VTOL wherever the required real estate is reasonably available.

The Air Bus

Air bus refers to a large capacity (200–300 passengers), relatively slow (400–600 mph) aircraft designed to operate over short to medium distances (150–500

---

1. And, perhaps eventually, freight, although the very short take-off and landing applications to date have been for small numbers of passengers. For example, the Helio Aircraft "Twin Stallion," can carry 17 people over a speed range of 40 to 300 miles per hour, using two 600 h.p. turbo-prop engines and having a gross weight of 9,300 pounds.

miles) on high density corridors or feeder routes. The Boston–New York–
Washington and the San Francisco–Los Angeles corridors for example, might be
suitable for air bus operations. Air bus type aircraft are in various states of development and production. The Lockheed L-1011 Tristar and the McDonnell-
Douglas DC-10 might be configurated, for example, to function as well as air
buses. Already under development at Lockheed and McDonnell-Douglas are
additional models such as twin-engine and convertible freighter-passenger
versions. McDonnell-Douglas is also examining all-cargo models.[2] The European
A-300B has been surrounded with controversy but is scheduled for production
in 1973. However, important economies will be realized only when large scale air
buses are carefully integrated with connecting transport systems, rapid loading
and unloading systems, and automated ticketing and baggage handling. VTOL or
STOL might find considerable application as the collection and distribution
mode within the total air bus system.

Large Subsonic Jets and the SST

Perhaps the most significant advance from a regional point of view is the development of large subsonic jets in a class with the military C-5A, the Boeing
747 and the Douglas DC-10.[3] Some idea of the differences in scale between these
and earlier jets is given in Table 5-1. The larger jets eventually may save 50 percent on operating costs for ranges greater than 1,000 miles.[4]

The large subsonic craft should provide not only greatly lowered passenger
transport costs between regions within the United States and from the United
States to foreign countries, but they should also, because of their size, be able to
use standard freight containers. The use of containers in itself would tend to lower
air freight costs and the use of standardized containers would greatly enhance
intermodal compatability.

Like other aircraft, the large subsonic jets have relatively great ability to get
into and out of locations isolated by geographic barriers. The existence of economical jet freighters with this capability could play a role in facilitating com-

---

2. For a summary discussion of the status of these different models, see "Cost Sharing
Proposed for A–300B Airbus," *Aviation Week and Space Technology,* June 2, 1969, p. 165.
For more recent information, see "A–300B Airbus Picks up Momentum," *Aviation Week,*
October 19, 1970, p. 28 and "British Veto BAC–311, A–300 B-7," *Aviation Week,*
December 7, 1970, p. 16

3. A recent general discussion is F. W. Kolk and D. R. Blundell, "Evolution and
Revolution with the Jumbo Trijets, *Astronautics & Aeronautics,* October 1968, p. 649.

4. For the increase in aircraft productivity in the late 1950s, see National Academy of
Sciences-National Research Council, *U.S. Transportation: Resources, Performance and
Problems* (Washington: NAS-NRC publication 841-S, 1961), p. 185. For example, the DC-7
had an available capacity of 2,700 ton-miles per hour, whereas the DC-8 has an available
capacity of 9,370 ton-miles per hour.

Table 5-1
Comparison of Load Capabilities of Large
Subsonic Jets with the Boeing 707

	Take-off Weight (000 lbs.)	Seats	Max. Payload (000 lbs.)	Range (mi.)
707–120	257	181	52	3200-4650
747 (Original)	710	490	178	5800
C-5A	730-760	750+[1]	220-265	3000-6500
DC-10 (short-med. haul)	410	345	80	300-2500
DC-10-30 (intercontinental)	555	345	111	6100
L-1011-1 (short-med. haul)	409	345	88	3300-3900
L-1011-8 (intercontinental)	595	400	100+	4600-7000

[1] Taken from "The Aeroplane," June 2, 1966.

Source: *Jane's All the World's Aircraft 1970-71*, Corrected to 1 August 1970, Jane's Yearbooks, London, England. 1971.

munications, and the growth of distant areas such as Alaska, Hawaii, and Puerto Rico. However, this aspect of air transport will probably have little importance for most U.S. regional development.

One cannot leave a discussion of air transport vehicles without considering the effect of the supersonic transport aircraft on regional economic development. Much controversy has arisen over the development of a U.S. supersonic transport. Federal funding has been suspended with the consequence that the Boeing development program has been stopped. Nevertheless, both the British-French Concorde and the Soviet Tupelov 144 are well along in their developments although both aircraft have been in some difficulty. The domestic controversy focuses on both environmental (noise and pollution) and government program priority (financing issues). At the present time, it appears highly unlikely that any supersonic aircraft will be permitted to fly over domestic land areas unless very successful means are found to eliminate the sonic boom. This would basically limit SST operation to coastal or near coastal areas of the country and would tend to favor the international and intracoastal trade of those areas.

The advantages of very high speed air services to inland areas could only be obtained directly if the sonic boom were tolerated or eliminated; if not, vehicle transfers or SST flight at uneconomic subsonic speeds would be required with their consequent increases in cost. These considerations suggest that the emergence of the SST may result in some disadvantages to inland regions.

Air Traffic Control

Advances in air traffic control have not entirely lived up to their earlier promise. Many potential capabilities have been known for some time, but their final implementation still requires considerably more effort.[5]

Before 1960, an all-weather, or "zero-zero" semi-automatic landing system was discussed and worked out technically, but it has not come into general use. Substantially more development is required for automatic air-ground communications, including computer control and integration of flight plans, clearances, and radar observations; the use of distance measuring equipment to reduce air space between planes in flight; and the sophisticated and integrated application of existing capabilities to achieve the benefits of automated or semi-automated airway operation.

The importance of air traffic control technology lies in the need to expand airway and terminal (e.g., runway) capacity. Part of the expansion will effectively come from larger aircraft, but much of it must come from improved control systems.

Rail Transportation

Recent improvements and technological changes in railroad operations appear dramatic. The reason, however, probably lies not in the changes themselves, but in the archaic image the railroads have projected until recently.

A brief catalog of the kinds of changes involved includes: improvements in power sources, drastic changes in the design and capacity of freight cars, improvements in passenger cars and, related to these, the spread of containerization and piggyback operations. Piggyback and containerization are particularly important as they promise a complete intermodal capability, that is, the shipment of goods from point to point in the world with minimal need for handling in transit.

A revolution in the modus operandi of the railroads is also underway. This is particularly evident in the organization and control of operations, communications, and information, all of which are closely related to the computer. Maintenance of way and equipment is another area which is showing substantial improvement. Finally, there are a host of commercial innovations underway, connected not only with piggyback and containerization, but also with, for example, the possibility of leasing equipment.

The commercial innovations are worth particular notice. They could allow for easier innovation and an increased interest in railroad R & D. These could lead to improvements in existing railroad technology and also to some major changes, such as automated container loading and the use of glideways. The railroad thus, potentially, can achieve greater regularity, greater intermodality, and greater utilization of inherent low line-haul cost capabilities. Yet, despite considerable publicity and a number of apparent changes, little is spent on railroad

---

5. See A. D'Arcy Harvey, "Air Traffic Control-Present and Future," in NAS-NRC, *U.S. Transportation.*

R & D. One basic reason is that user industries in general tend to leave research to their suppliers. Another factor discouraging interest in innovation is the mutual interdependence and enforced standardization between roads. The government until recently has also paid relatively little attention to railroad development.

Power

The replacement of steam locomotives with diesels, which started about 1935, has been essentially completed. The result has been lower costs: lower maintenance costs, lower truck costs, and an estimated 50 percent decrease in motive power costs.[6]

Future motive power possibilities include gas turbines, turbo-jets for high speed passenger runs, and nuclear power.[7] More readily applicable changes are the use of hydraulic torque converters for the diesel-electric engine and the distribution of electricity to give individual cars along the train motive power, thus reducing the problems of slack and train size. A turbo-electric locomotive could in this manner give perhaps 10,000 and 12,000 h.p. with a considerable saving in dead weight.[8]

Other potential power advances are the use of linear synchronous electric motors such as those discussed in connection with high-speed inter-urban transit, and solid state switching devices, which make possible a brushless d.c. motor. All of these could lead to changes as important as those created by the introduction of large diesels.

Communications, Data Processing, and Control

Computers and radio equipment have made possible the effective operation of unit trains and the better utilization of large investments in specialized equip-

---

6. Ray McBrian, "Atomic Power — Why It Must Be Studied," *Progressive Railroading*, Vol. 9, No. 2 (March-April, 1966). Steam locomotive repair costs during their heyday (the late 1930s) were 6.5% of gross revenue, while diesel costs are 4.5%. With larger diesels, perhaps 2,500–5,000 h.p. compared to the 1300 h.p. of most of todays stock, repair costs might be cut to 2.5% of gross revenue. See also Burton N. Behling, "Railroads — Their Development, Problems, and Prospects;" in National Academy of Sciences-National Research Council, *U.S. Transportation*. The number of diesels is also less — 29,000 in 1959 compared to the maximum of 68,000 steam engines in 1920, while revenue ton-miles hauled has increased. This suggests that most of the maintenance savings stem from increased power of the diesel, rather than lower per engine costs.

7. For example SNAP-4, which could give 2,000 to 3,000 h.p. in a nuclear locomotive. Shielding is a problem, however.

8. Ray McBrian, "New Motive Power Technology;" in Robert S. Nelson and Edward M. Johnson, eds. *Technological Change and the Future of the Railways* (Evanston: Transportation Center at Northwestern University, 1961). This article gives a catalog of some of the motive power changes that are underway or contemplated.

ment. Computers have been used not only in systems analysis of entire railroads and, at the other extreme, to mechanize clerical tasks, but also to gain a highly intensified use of existing facilities and equipment. For example, without tight scheduling and excellent information on car locations, the use of specialized cars would be uneconomical because utilization would be too low. At a general level, an increased information capacity aids rail management in making more rational and effective decisions and, through sophisticated inventory control and equipment management, can give marked cost reductions. Better information on car locations and route and arrival schedules also lowers shippers' costs, and so makes rail rates more competitive. Computerization could also reduce the boxcar inventories required at intermediate stops, which would tend to make improved service to small and remote localities more economical.

Communications and automation are also yielding major improvements in the following areas:

a. Automatic classification yards. Cars can be uncoupled and humped, tracks selected by push-button, and engines controlled, all with a minimum of human intervention. Losses and damage are cut down and the whole operation greatly speeded up.

b. Electronic communications using microwaves, TV and facsimile, make it possible to use automatic systems for control, hot-box detection, weighing and car identification, and general management information processing.

c. With good communications, computers, and systems synthesis and analysis capability, efficiency and effectiveness in overall operations become possible with sizeable potential gains. The possibility of planning, simulating, and making long-term forecasts can allow optimization of equipment usage and the elimination of many costly aberrations in internal allocations. Unit train operations become feasible, and overall higher utilization can be obtained. As a small example of the sort of results that could be achieved, a 50 percent increase in car utilization would give an effective addition of about 78,000 cars to class I railroads,[9] which, in turn, would achieve substantial capital cost savings. An overall computerized management system could provide analysis of traffic for rate, service, and operating decisions; information for management and shippers on location, routes, and arrivals of shipments and cars; optimization of train scheduling and consist; equipment and inventory control; profitability analysis of activities and departments; as well as personnel and active accounting and billing functions; and automatic car identification.

Unit Trains and Integral-Train Operations

The unit train moves as one complete unit from its origin to its destination. This saves considerably on classification costs. The unit train can be used when-

---

9. Estimated from data taken from *U.S. Statistical Abstract.*

ever there is substantial tonnage to be moved regularly from one point to another. The principle was originally developed for coal, but it is now used for grain, aluminum, iron ore, sugar, and other commodities as well. There are also "liner trains" which carry high priority freight on a regular basis.[10]

The savings in direct line-haul costs from the use of unit trains is estimated at up to 50 percent. But for unit trains to be economical, long-term scheduling and good demand forecasts are required. The customer saves in the reliability of delivery, where speed is a bit less important than regularity. Basically, economies in the use of integral trains require a radical improvement in load factors, the ability to make long run predictions of car use, and good loading systems.[11]

The unit train may be particularly significant for regional development because many depressed areas depend on the export of such bulk raw materials as coal, iron ore, and timber. The lower costs offered by unit train operation will improve, first of all, the competitive position of inland producers of these materials. Second, lower transport costs will make the materials themselves more competitive. For example, unit trains could reduce the delivered price of coal, which would increase its attractiveness as a power source relative to other fossil fuels or nuclear power.

Special Cars

Specialized cars, such as the Big John hopper, have been developed for a number of purposes.[12] Individual cars, designed for easy loading and unloading, can carry larger loads at lower rates, and roller bearing and cushion underframes cut damage losses. The riding qualities of general purpose cars have also been considerably improved. Special cushioning and insulation and increased size and weight have given cars greater effectiveness and provide much better protection for cargo.

Specialized cars, in effect, are developed for the shipper rather than for the railroads; but both the shipper and the railroads save on costs. The extent to which railroad cost savings will be passed on in the form of lower rates depends, of course, partly on regulatory decisions. But innovations such as specialized cars do provide an impetus for lower rates, and by linking rates more closely to costs, eventually may revolutionize rate making.

----

10. See, for example, John R. Southgate, "Liner Trains are Now Underway," *Transport World*, January, 1966, which describes the British Railroad's London to Glasgow run. The trains are "booked" and carry 40 27-foot long prearranged containers. The payload is 6,750 tons, and a train runs each night.

11. See, for example, Cripes in *Railroad Equipment Strategy* and also *Integral Trains* (Railroad Systems and Management Association, Chicago, 1963).

12. For some examples of special cars, see p. 106 of *Railroad Equipment Strategy*.

Piggyback and Containerization

TOFC (trailer-on-flat-car), or piggyback, as it is generally called, by whatever arrangement of trailer ownership, involves the carriage on a railroad of a road
trailer. By extending the geographic range and door-to-door quality of rail-
oriented services, piggyback has allowed the railroad to penetrate new markets.
In 1969, however, piggyback accounted for only about 5 percent of all carloadings
on class I railroads and, although the use of piggyback has been growing rapidly,
it still accounts for only a small part of total car loadings.[13]

More broadly conceived, however, piggyback involves the movement of a
container by both road and rail, and so is an intermediate stage in the progress
towards standardized containerization and uninhibited intermodal flows.

Piggyback achieves significant economies in terminal operations, fewer steps
in handling freight and a reduction in classification at origin and destination.
Containers may promise even more advantages than trailers such as lower clearances, lower centers of gravity, and lower capital costs, and they are much more
suitable for intermodal movements. Containers can also be used for storage, with
built-in refrigeration if necessary. They can be stacked up, and could be handled
by automatic container loading equipment. Thus, for those journeys which involve numerous interfaces, containerization could have a distinct overall price
advantage.

Piggyback service can be provided economically at lower volumes than
those required for economical rail operation. This, and the general ubiquity of
highways, imply that piggyback may substantially improve the service available
in the smaller regional centers and remote areas.

Physical Plant and Its Maintenance

Considerable savings have been achieved in the construction and maintenance of rail plant. Welding rail joints has reduced maintenance-of-way costs, as
have lowering grades, straightening curves, technical improvements in ties, heavier
rails, better metallurgy, and mechanized maintenance of way. For example, the
use of specialized equipment for pre-tieing rails and ties can yield large savings.

Highway Transportation

By far the most important change in highway technology in the post-war
era, ranking alongside the diesel train and the jet airplane in its significance, is the

---

13. Transportation Association of America, "Transportation Facts and Trends"
Quarterly Supplement, January 1971

Interstate Highway System. Vehicle technology, however, has seen no innovation in the post-World War II period of comparable importance. The vehicle has, rather, improved gradually and uniformly, with the total change in technology given by the sum of many small changes, rather than dominated by one or two major innovations. In the immediate future, vehicle technology will probably continue to experience only minor improvements. However, major innovations have been proposed, and in the somewhat more distant future these could prove revolutionary.

Vehicle Design

Trucking costs generally decline with increasing truck capacity.[14] The savings which can be achieved by increasing truck size, however, are limited by both vehicle and highway surface technology. Larger trucks generally imply an increased axle load, and hence require a stronger, more expensive surface, and, in addition, obviously require more surface area if the same level of service is to be maintained. Apart from any consideration of the highway itself, the possible size of trucks, especially truck trains, is limited by the relatively limited capability of the truck's guidance system.

Two strictly technological innovations have been suggested. The first is the gas turbine engine. The major economy of gas turbines comes from fuel savings, as a turbine can run efficiently on a wide variety of fuels, including very cheap ones.[15] The second possible innovation is the introduction of ground effect machines (GEMs). Ground effect vehicles, if they become economical, could replace the truck. The greatest potential savings offered by the GEMs are reduced right of way costs as they could even be operated on a smooth, grass surface. GEMs would encounter the same difficulties with congestion as do current trucks and automobiles. Their speed capability is somewhat higher (and so control systems would have to be better), but there remain considerable technological difficulties in the control of acceleration and deceleration.[16]

---

14. Walter Y. Oi and Arthur P. Hurter, *Economics of Private Truck Transportation* (Dubuque, Iowa: William C. Brown Co. for the Transportation Center at Northwestern University, 1965) p. 186. See also M.L. Burstein, A. Victor Cabot, John W. Egan, Arthur P. Hurter and Stanley Warner, *The Cost of Trucking: Econometric Analysis* (Dubuque, Iowa: William C. Brown Co. for the Transportation Center at Northwestern University, 1965).

15. John R. Meyer, John F. Kain, and Martin Wohl, *The Urban Transportation Problem* (Cambridge: Harvard University Press, 1965) p. 318. Chapter 12 is a good discussion of the role of technology in urban transportation.

16. For some GEM applications see Meil Harrison, "Mass Transit Assessment," *Flight International*, Dec. 30, 1965 and W. B. Caisley, "A Mode-Mixing Multi-Part," *Flight International*, May 19, 1966.

Highway Surface Design and Organization

The costs of trucking depend on both the quality of the highway surface and the degree of congestion. It is immediately obvious that the costs of trucking over a poor road can be reduced by improving the surface and, similarly, where congestion is substantial, trucking costs can be reduced by adding highway capacity.

In more general terms, cost savings could perhaps be achieved by designing special truck highways. On links with a considerable volume of trucking, for example, separate lanes might be reserved for trucks.[17] This innovation would reduce the costs of lanes for passenger travel, where a thinner surface would suffice, and generally decrease congestion for both trucks and automobiles. However, it would also place the entire burden of truck highways on trucking firms instead of just the incremental costs of the additional surface required to make a highway suitable for trucks, as is currently the case.[18] Unless the volume of truck travel along the truck highways was substantial, this could mean higher average costs.

A somewhat similar, although less radical proposal, has been advanced for urban arterials. Intersections cause the major time loss in arterial urban travel. To mitigate this problem "Bantam Expressways" have been proposed.[19] A Bantam Expressway is taken to be a road with characteristics lying somewhere between those of a major urban arterial and a freeway. The Bantamway would have lanes reserved for trucks and buses, and underpasses for through automobile traffic at intersections. Trucks and buses would cross intersections on grade, but the decrease in congestion allowed by the underpass, would increase the effective speed of both automobiles and trucks.

Signaling and Control

Perhaps the most advanced and readily applicable technological possibilities for highways lie in electronic control devices. Several cities are currently experimenting with computerized control of stop lights at intersections. New York City, for example, currently has 430 intersections, about 5 percent of the total,

---

17. This solution has generally been advanced for urban bus transit, e.g., by Meyer, et al., op. cit., but it could also be applied to trucks on high density routes.

18. See John R. Meyer, Merton J. Peck, John Stenason, Charles Zwick, *The Economics of Competition in the Transportation Industries* (Cambridge: Harvard University Press, 1959) Chapter IV.

19. Herman L. Danforth and William P. Sheldon, "Bantam Expressway — New Urban Face of the Future," *Traffic Quarterly*, Vol. 20, No. 3 (July, 1966).

controlled. The project hopes to have an additional 1,000 intersections controlled
by the end of 1972 and a total of 7,000 controlled by the late 1970s. The New
York system uses overhead ultrasonic detectors to measure traffic flows, and a
centralized computer system to control the stop lights. A similar project is underway in Toronto, and TV is being used to monitor traffic on the John C. Lodge
Freeway in Detroit and on the Houston Gulf Freeway in Texas. Detroit found
that the use of a computer to control traffic shortened the duration of rush hour
congestion, although not the degree of congestion during the peak.[20]

The computer systems in use to date rely on the traditional stop light. The
basic idea is to gather data continuously, and use these data to optimize traffic
flows by manipulating signals. The same basic philosophy can, however, be
extended to more revolutionary signaling devices. It has been suggested, for example, that usual signs be supplemented or supplanted by verbal messages trans-
mitted automatically to vehicles. Computer technology is presently insufficiently
advanced to allow flexible voice communications, but its potentiality for increasing
safety and routing traffic is obvious, and simple, standard messages could be
handled with existing equipment.

The logical culmination of signaling advances is the fully automated highway.
The individual driver would retain control of his vehicle before and after the line-
haul portion of the trip. During the line-haul portion, however, control of the
vehicle would rest with a computerized guidance system. A "first generation"
automated highway could be built with current technology. The costs, however,
would probably be very high, and the possible performance characteristics will be
less than when more advanced computers and other control mechanisms are
developed. But such a system, when it is implemented, could greatly increase
highway utilization and safety.[21] The major application of automated highways
would probably be in megalopolitan areas, where traffic volumes are sufficient
to realize the potential scale economies.

20. Harry Vaughn, "What is New in Traffic Control," *Nations Cities*, Vol. 4, No. 1
(July, 1966). For a fairly technical report of the Houston Gulf Freeway experience, see
Charles Pinnell, "Gulf Freeway Surveillance and Control Project," *Traffic Quarterly*, Vol.
20, No. 1 (Jan., 1966). For a Syracuse experience, see "A Computerized Traffic Control
System for Any City," *The American City*, July, 1966. For a more technical discussion
of particular control devices see Highway Research Record No. 105, *Traffic Control:
Devices and Delineation – 7 Reports* (Washington: Highway Research Board, 1966), and
Highway Research Record No. 118, *Statistical and Mathematical Aspects of Traffic – 6
Reports* (Washington: Highway Research Board, 1966).

21. See John R. Meyer, John F. Kain and Martin Wohl, *Technology and Urban Transportation*, Report prepared for the White House Panel on Civilian Technology, July, 1962,
Chapter V, which also discusses signaling and control devices. For a discussion of a current
experiment with an automated highway, see *The Reporter* (American Public Works Asso-
ciation) Vol. 32, No. 8 (Aug., 1965). Also see R. L. Cosgriff, J. J. English and W. B. Roeca,
"An Automatic System for Longitudinal Control of Individual Vehicles," Highway Research
Record No. 122, *Road User Characteristics – 9 Reports* (Washington: Highway Research
Board, 1966) is a technical discussion of a guidance system.

Waterways

Two important changes are underway in maritime technology. The first is the improvement in port activities and the second, more fundamentally technical in nature, is the development of air-cushion vehicles or hovercraft.

The improvement in port technology is connected with containerization and in fact is largely based upon it. Containerization has brought about a decrease in transfer time, less damage and theft, smaller storage requirements, a reduction in administration and paperwork, and, fundamentally, a decreased port investment requirement because the same port can handle more cargo. Reduced turn-around time would tend to make small ports more economical as transshipment points, with no substantial increase in capital requirement. Containerization may, however, require redesigned port facilities.[22]

Not all cargo is physically suitable for containers, nor is the expense for cargo that is suitable always justified. But in many cases, containerization can give large economies of scale, and a considerable increase in investment in the technology of container handling will be required in the future.

The reductions in terminal costs which containers generally achieve could substantially increase the use of both barges and seaports. For example, a 7-day California–New York-via-Panama Canal container service is planned. In general, containers tend to reduce the high terminal costs of water transportation while not substantially increasing water's low line-haul costs. Where it is already an alternative, water transport could for these reasons become more competitive with the other modes.

Contracts to develop a 100-ton hovercraft have been let by the Navy and Marad in hopes that it could be a prototype for 4,000-5,000 ton ships. The research and developments costs for developing such large hovercraft are sizeable. A team set up by the Department of Commerce to determine the feasibility of surface-effect cargo ships concluded that for a vessel of 5,000 tons gross, it would take 5 years and $70 million to develop a preliminary engineering design. If a technology could be developed, however, the hovercraft could eliminate the need for many port facilities because of its ability to go from land to water at a large number of locations, thus permitting water transportation service at a large number of locations along a waterway without substantial port facility investment.

Pipelines

Continuing technological progress in the use of pipelines is to be expected, but it is unlikely that the next decade will see any innovation which will particu-

22. See Donald Shoup, "Port Operation and Economic Development" (Doctoral dissertation, Harvard University, 1966).

larly revolutionize their operation. Automation is proceeding in communication, operation of valves, and telemetering of gauges. Measuring advances, such as the use of isotopes to mark the division between batches of fluid throughputs have been made, and computers are being used to optimize pipeline design and operation. Pipelines also have an increasing ability to transport solids, despite the difficulties of preparing the fluids and reclaiming the solids. There has been some pipeline transportation of iron ore, nickel sludges, limestone, coal and over short distances, of grains in suspension. Containers are also a possibility for pipelines, although economical methods have not yet been proposed.

There has been a general decrease in the costs of both laying and constructing pipelines. The use of larger diameters, for example, gives greater capacity for nearly the same cost, and automatic building on-site from premanufactured coils could cut costs tremendously.[23]

Summary and Conclusions

Table 5–2 summarizes recent trends in mode technology, and lists qualitatively the direct effects of these changes. Three broad themes run through the technological changes occurring in all the modes. First, computers and other automatic data-processing and control equipment are being applied to the problems of plan-

Table 5–2
Effects of Technological Change in the Various Modes

Mode	Technological Change	Performance & Cost Effect
	V/STOL Advances	door-to-door time for passengers and high value cargo greatly reduced
	Air Bus	increased speed and decreased cost for medium range passenger trips
Air	Large Subsonic Jets	substantial line haul cost savings compared with today's costs, so demand will increase; size makes intermodal containers more feasible
	SST	all regions in close communication with distant areas
	Air traffic control and enroute automation	increased capacity at metropolitan airports

---

23. See Gorden C. Locke, "The Oil Pipeline Industry," in NAS-NRC, *U. S. Transportation*, and K. L. Burke in *Ekistics*, Vol. 16, No. 92 (July, 1963).

Table 5–2, continued

Mode	Technological Change	Performance & Cost Effect
Rail	Power scale up, power costs down 1. large diesels 2. power for each car 3. new propulsion technology	lower line-haul direct operating and maintenance costs
	Communication and Automation 1. management planning and equipment utilization 2. unit and integral trains 3. yard technology	lower overall costs due to improved utilization and control, greater integral and unit train possibilities, lower terminal and yard costs
	Containerization and Piggyback	lower terminal costs; increased regularity
	Cars 1. special purpose cars 2. cushioning bearings	lower damage costs; speed and cost savings in loading; lower terminal costs; increased shipper convenience.
	Maintenance of way and construction	overall line-haul costs down; point-to-point speed improved
Road	Automation	line-haul costs down; improved safety
	Containerization and piggyback	terminal costs down
	Multi-truck units	line-haul costs down
	Air-cushion vehicles, potential	increased speed, decreased roadbed costs
Pipelines	Lower construction costs	reduced line-haul costs for bulk commodities
	Automatic control and computerization	
Waterways	Containerization	lower terminal costs, giving increased advantage to low line-haul costs
	Ship and port redesign	

ning, managerial decision making, and the operating problems of the particular modes. Second, various forms of containerization and their auxiliary equipment are becoming more widespread, although the implementation of these innovations is advancing somewhat slower than might be desirable. Finally, vehicle operating characteristics and potentials are being improved.

On a very general level, the changes in mode technology promise decreased overall costs, increased regularity, greater intermodal compatability, increased speed, and greater safety. It is impossible to foresee the ultimate impact of these changes in any detail. It is possible, however, to indicate some major implications.

Effect of Absolutely Declining Transport Costs

All of the technological changes listed above promise lower costs to the operators of the modes. The degree to which these are passed on to shippers through lower rates depends, of course, to a large extent on regulatory actions. It is safe to presume, however, that transport rates will decline in the coming years.

Absolutely lower transportation rates immediately imply that transportation is likely to become relatively less important in industrial location decisions. In concrete terms, this means that natural transportation advantages, such as a location at a seaport or railroad junction point, should decrease relative to other locational parameters, such as the availability of labor and the proximity of markets.

This conclusion is strengthened by the increasing ubiquity of the transport system. A system of standardized containers, which would insure complete intermodal capability could result in a highly efficient door-to-door freight transport system. This would tend to reduce the competitive disadvantage of the small shipper, and tend to eliminate natural transport advantages which some locations have. The transport system is also in a sense becoming more divisible, as well as more highly integrated.

Relatively Declining Long-haul Costs

Many of the technological changes discussed above serve primarily to decrease terminal costs. This is particularly evident in containerization, piggyback, and in some of the automatic control devices used by the railroads in their yard operations. The cost impact of these innovations will be felt primarily by the railroads and waterways, which currently have high terminal costs and low line-haul costs. From one point of view, reducing the terminal costs of these modes will make them optimal modes for somewhat shorter distances than is currently the case, or, to be very specific, truck-rail competition will increase for short hauls. However, the major impact of reducing terminal costs will be to increase the utilization of modes having inherently low line-haul costs, and it might increase the locational attraction of raw material sources.

Other chapters have noted qualifications on the trend towards centralization, and these need not be repeated here. Technology, however, is not uniformly on the side of decreasing long-haul costs.

The past decreases in short-haul costs introduced by trucking will probably continue. Cost reductions can be achieved by improvements in truck technology, segregating trucks on separate rights-of-way, or in some cases simply by building more or better roads. More dramatic reductions might be achieved by automated highways and by the introduction of ground effect vehicles. V/STOL aircraft also hold considerable promise for increasing short-haul speeds, and possibly reducing short-haul costs.

The Effect of Increased Speed

Developments in air technology are definitely reducing the costs of long-haul air freight transport. The costs of air freight, however, are unlikely to become competitive with rail and water for many years. It seems best, therefore, to regard developments in air transportation primarily as increases in speed and as potentially competitive, if at all, with existing long-haul truck services.

An increase in speed widens a market area, and so promotes centralization, just as does a decrease in long-haul costs. The prime example is undoubtedly perishable vegetables. This aspect of air freight, however, applies to any relatively high-value or perishable commodity. The examples of such commodities now are rather rare, so air freight should not be very important in the short to middle run. The mix of products, however, seems to be shifting towards such commodities, so air freight may have considerable long run significance.

The immediate importance of air passenger transport may be somewhat greater. The increasing speed and declining relative cost of air travel could lead to a decentralization in some service industries. For these industries the availability of technical consulting and general communications is important, but with the increasing capabilities of air travel, their availability at any one point could become less critical in attracting service industries.[24]

General Conclusions

Technological changes, as they affect the competitive position of particular modes, seem to be, at least in part, offsetting. Containerization, for example is reducing the costs of water transportation, while various computer applications and specialized procedures such as the unit train are reducing railroad costs. Thus, technological change, in net, will probably not make the rails more competitive with water than they are now. Similarly, long-haul costs are falling, but technological advances can also reduce short-haul costs, leaving the relative long-haul, short-haul price configuration unchanged.

---

24. Daniel Shimshoni, "Aspects of Scientific Entreprenuership," (Unpublished doctoral dissertation, Harvard University, June, 1966).

In general, technological change does not indicate any great change in the competitive positions of the various modes. Technological changes will alter the cost picture primarily by generally reducing all transportation costs.

The general trend of technological change also suggests that the transportation system will become more ubiquitous and more flexible. Piggyback, for example, is at once economical for smaller volumes and able to utilize both highways and rail lines, which makes it more ubiquitous than unadorned railroad transportation. A standardized system of containerization is certainly the next step. Full implementation of the container principle would provide a much more uniform and extensive transport system. It would, in effect, tend to make all modes available to any location, although some rate and service differentials would persist. Air transportation is of course also capable of considerable ubiquity, largely because no special surface is required and small aircraft can be relatively economical to operate.

The overall impact of technological change suggests that the importance of transportation in locational decisions will decline. Some of the innovations currently underway are directly applicable to development problems. V/STOL aircraft, for example, may be very useful in metropolitan regions and, for another, unit trains may have an impact on regions which export bulk commodities. However, the trends in technology indicate that it will be increasingly true that providing a region with a superior transportation system will be of little value unless the region is also attractive for other reasons.

6

The Impact of Transportation Regulation and Practices on Regional Development

Regulation of transportation principally involves controls over rates, entry into the market, and the service characteristics or other conditions of non-price competition. Ancillary to these are controls over such matters as financial affairs, labor relations, record keeping, and the provision of information. Each of these to some extent has its own particular purpose. The overall goal of transportation regulation is usually presumed to be promotion of the optimum allocation of resources within the economy; of course, in reality the goals might be much more complex, or less singular than this and often conflicting as well.

General Considerations

Principles of Transportation Pricing

As a general rule, the allocation of resources within an economy will, all other things equal, be better if the price of each commodity is set equal to the costs of producing the last unit, or, in more technical language, if prices are set equal to marginal costs. As this general rule is as applicable to transportation as to any other service or commodity, economists initially presume that transportation rates should be set equal to the marginal costs of providing the service.

There are, however, difficulties which may warrant a departure from the marginal cost rule in practice. In particular, the advantages of marginal cost pricing depend critically on the validity of certain assumptions which may not be well met in the real world. Moreover, marginal cost pricing is primarily a static concept with potentially adverse financial, incentive and investment aspects.

Current Practice

Whatever the merits, regulatory agencies have to an important extent ignored costs in establishing regulated rates. This is particularly evident in the rail rates historically set by the Interstate Commerce Commission (ICC). In many cases, the ICC has used the "value of commodity" principle, and set rates in relation to the prices or value of goods to be transported. This could be justified if:
(1) service costs varied directly with commodity value; or (2) if demand for rail

service varied directly with commodity value. There is limited reason at best for believing that either of these conditions has much validity under modern circumstances.

Pursuit of the value of commodity principle in railroad pricing has had important economic consequences. Its application has produced rates on bulk commodities which are generally closely related to long-run marginal costs, and rates on manufactures that are substantially greater. This rail rate structure has influenced the allocation of traffic, and hence of resources, among the modes. For example from the point of view of the shipper of high value manufactured goods, the truck has often become the cheapest alternative, even over fairly long distances. But the costs of trucking in many cases are greater than the costs of rail for some of these distances and commodities. If the rail rate structure were rationalized to bring rates into line with costs, the lowest or competitive tariff range of the truck would decline and, from a general point of view, the same quantity of goods could be transported for a smaller amount of resources.

Rail rates also have had an impact on the regional distribution of activity. High rail rates on manufactures have produced a relative decrease in shippers' intraregional as contrasted with interregional distribution costs through truck substitution. And, as has been explained elsewhere in this report, relatively cheap short haul costs promote industrial decentralization.

The Prospect

The trend in regulation is definitely toward a cost-based pricing principle. This trend, if it fully materializes, almost surely would lower the price of transporting manufactures by rail, and might increase the price of moving bulk and some "low-rated" agricultural commodities. Insofar as transport costs have any locational leverage, this would tend to promote industrial centralization, and possibly at sites closer to raw material sources.

Historical Effect of Regulation and Practices on Regional Growth

Intrastate-Interstate Rate Relationships

Early mercantilist policies in several states promoted local jobbing and manufacturing by rates that favored intrastate shippers. These, in turn, often led to the curtailment of growth of like economic enterprises in neighboring states. A classic example was the sharp reduction in intrastate rates on fresh fish from Mobile to Birmingham and other Alabama points which nullified the comparative advantage of Pensacola, Florida in supplying fish to Alabama markets. Another case involved Minnesota's action in fixing reduced maximum rates on general mer-

chandise and some commodities that handicapped border points in adjacent
states from developing their jobbing business. The best-known instance was that
of Texas, where a graded-and-maximum intrastate rate structure, designed to
encourage uniform commercial, industrial, and agricultural development throughout the state, resulted in discrimination against Shreveport, Louisiana in its
rivalry for Texas business against Texas jobbing points.[1] It was this situation that
led to the Shreveport doctrine upholding ICC authority to order the cessation
of discrimination against a locality outside of a state engendered by a disparity in
rates.

Existing law, strengthened by amendment as recently as 1958, gives the
ICC ample power to raise intrastate railway rates to remove discriminations in
particular interstate rivalries and burdens cast on interstate commerce by intrastate rate levels yielding insufficient revenues to support a carrier's costs. The aid
of the ICC can be enlisted readily by communities and shippers who suffer
injury on account of discriminatory intrastate rates. Conversely though, no relief
will be offered by the ICC where intrastate shippers are prejudiced in having to
pay higher rates than competing interstate shippers. It should be noted, also, that
the ICC is specifically precluded from exercising power over intrastate rates of
motor and water carriers. The Civil Aeronautics Board (CAB), it would appear,
could possibly exercise authority over discriminatory intrastate airline fares and
rates but has not done so. In general, there has been little investigation of
interstate-intrastate rate relationships and the problems that exist, if any, within
the non-rail modes.

Lower Rates for Long than for Short Hauls

Individual examples of charging more for a shorter than for a longer haul,
owing to competition at the more distant points and to the circuity of routes,
have been fairly common. Indeed, in the Southern and Mountain-Pacific territories*, the practice developed historically into what might be termed a system
of rate-making.[2]

In the South, cities located on the Atlantic seaboard and at the fall-line of
navigable rivers were made basing points because of actual or potential water
competition. Interior cities like Atlanta were also made basing points because of
railroad and market competition. Rail rates to non-competitive points were constructed by adding local rates to basing point rates, with the result that the rate
pattern often was highly irregular and discriminatory against intermediate points.

---

1. Stuart Daggett, *Principles of Inland Transportation*, 4th ed. (New York: Harper and
Brothers, 1955), pp. 575–586.

*See Figure 6–1 for a map of the rate making territories.

2. Daggett, op. cit., pp. 398–404.

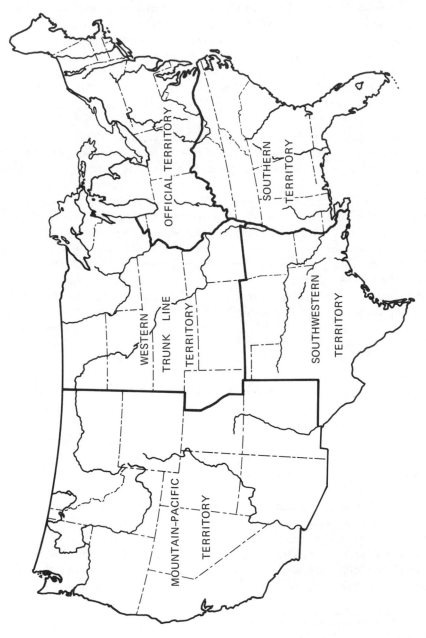

Figure 6-1. Railroad Rate Territories.

ICC action over a long period (since 1910) has largely substituted a mileage basis for the basing point system.

Similarly, intercoastal water competition influenced the construction of transcontinental rates in that rates to terminal cities on the Pacific Coast were sometimes established at a lower level than those to the non-competitive intermountain cities. Rates to the interior points were not uniformly the sum of the terminal plus the local rate back, but the differentials were frequently large. Initial ICC action (1911) to alleviate the discrimination against the intermountain points was to graduate the rate differences directly with the availability of water transport at midwestern and eastern origins and destinations. With the decline of water competition during the World War I years, the ICC in 1917 ordered the elimination of all rate disparities. In doing so, the railroads raised their terminal rates to the level of their intermountain rates, thus creating a blanket that extended several hundred miles from the Pacific Coast. Despite repeated applications by the railroads since then, the Commission has allowed relief on only a few commodities. One of the chief reasons prompting the Commission to deny the reinstallation of the old rate system has been the adverse effect of rate disparities on the growth of jobbing and industrial activity in the intermountain region. Under the mileage scales of the recently adopted uniform class rate structure, the locational advantage of the intermountain cities in terms of distance is given further protection.

Discrimination Against Regions

Alleged geographic discrimination affecting entire rate territories or regions, especially the South, was a major topic of investigation and controversy in the 1930s and 1940s.[3] Congress acknowledged the problem in 1940 when it outlawed undue prejudice against regions or territories. The matter was investigated by the ICC in Class Rate Investigation, 1939.[4] The record in this case shows that class rates were substantially higher in Southern and all other territories than in Official (Northeastern) Territory and that interterritorial rates between Official and the other territories were also substantially higher than in Official Territory. These disparities, in the opinion of the Commission, were a distinct competitive disadvantage to manufacturers in other (non-official) territories seeking to market products in the great consuming markets of the Northeast or Official Territory. Their disadvantage of location vis-à-vis manufacturers in Official Territory was accentuated by the additional burden of higher rates. Exhaustive cost studies in-

---

3. See, for example, Board of Investigation and Research, Transportation Act of 1940, *Summary Report on Study of Interterritorial Freight Rates* (Washington, March 30, 1943); Tennessee Valley Authority, *The Interterritorial Freight Rate Problem of the United States* (75th Cong., 1st sess., House Document No. 264, Washington, 1937).

4. *Class Rate Investigation, 1939*, 262 ICC 447 (1945).

dicated that there was "little significant difference" in the cost of rendering transportation service in the South as compared to the East. On the basis of cost and other transportation factors as well as the adverse effect on growth of manufactures, undue prejudice was declared to exist. To ameliorate the discriminations an interim increase of 10 percent in Eastern class rates and a 10 percent reduction in other territories were ordered, but the eventual solution was the ordering of complete uniformity in class rates effective in 1952. Any locational disadvantage would not be dissipated under the uniform mileage scales, but the uniform level of rates would be helpful to the more distant producers.

The existence of discrimination with respect to the all-important commodity rates was not ascertained. While the general levels of commodity rates in Southern and Official territories could not be compared for lack of data, lower rates in the South on many commodities were noted. The ICC did not accept the contention that lower rates on industrial raw materials in the South offset the disadvantage of higher class rates.

Atlantic Port Differentials

The Commission's adherence to distance as a test in determining undue prejudice has not always prevailed. The ICC refused to allow railways serving the northern tier ports of New York, Boston, Albany, and Portland to reduce rates on export and import traffic moving between these ports and so-called differential territory in the interior. The purpose of the lower rates was to eliminate the long-established differentials favoring the southern tier ports of Philadelphia, Baltimore, and Hampton Roads. These differentials had been agreed upon by the port railways as a compromise to avoid rate wars in 1877. Similar differentials on domestic traffic had been eliminated in 1930. Owing to differences in ocean freight rates (based on distance) prevailing at the time, the effect was to place all of the ports on a roughly equal basis with respect to combined rail and ocean charges. Subsequently, ocean rates to Europe and the United Kingdom were equalized to all ports. But Philadelphia and Baltimore continued to enjoy the advantage of the differential rates. The ICC declined to remove them largely because of the distance disadvantage of the northern tier ports. When reviewed by the courts, however, the ICC's holding of no undue prejudice was found erroneous because insufficient weight had been given to the interests of shippers and carriers and differences in distance had not been related to the costs and value of service of the competing railroads.[5] The reluctance of the Commission to allow competitive factors to upset a long-standing rate relationship is understandable. Since combined ocean and rail costs will probably vary little as among the

---

5. Boston and Maine v. United States, 202 F. Supp. (D. Mass. 1962); 373 U.S. 372 (1963).

competing ports, there should be little inefficiency induced by this practice of rate equalization.

The Impact of Regulation on the Pattern of Regional Comparative Advantages

Concentrating only on the railroad and ignoring intermodal competition, it may be surmised that regulation has fostered the development of regional resources, presumably along lines of comparative advantage, by eliminating geographic discrimination in rates. In the same vein, it should be noted that railways have been restrained from maintaining unreasonably high rates to offset or neutralize the natural advantages of location of shippers or communities and thus curb their competition and growth.[6] The abolition of personal discrimination may also have made a contribution to achieving comparative advantage to the extent that favored shippers were concentrated in a particular region.

Regulatory power over rates has only occasionally been asserted in a *positive* manner to influence the location of economic activity.[7] It has, however, acquiesced in the establishment of rate patterns, namely in response to competitive pressures by the carriers themselves, that have had pronounced regional impacts. (Some of these are described subsequently in this chapter.) Furthermore, the regulatory authorities have developed a strong reluctance to disrupt these patterns of regional preference once they have been established (as, for example, in the Atlantic ports case just discussed).

Under any structure of rates, even the most rational, there will be some actual or potential producers who will be excluded from markets owing to their disadvantages in location or cost of production. Such disadvantages sometimes may be overcome by freight rate reductions and carriers serving them may *voluntarily* adjust rates below a normal level for just such purposes. The ICC normally has not compelled carriers to make such reductions. Where rate adjustments are imposed on carriers, they usually must be based on transportation conditions and costs and not on the commercial needs of shippers, localities, or regions. If the Commission were to force rate adjustments to allow rival producers and regions to enter and to share markets, it would not only be assuming a role of arbiter of economic destinies but it would be involving itself in interregional political conflicts. In one of the famous and highly controversial Lake Cargo Coal Cases, involving essentially the rate differential between the northern and southern coal fields on lake-cargo coal, the Commission said: "We have neither the inclina-

---

6. D. Philip Locklin, *Economics of Transportation*, 6th ed. (Homewood, Ill.: Richard D. Irwin, 1966), p. 447.

7. Locklin, op. cit., pp. 445–447. See also Emery Troxel, *Economics of Transportation* (New York: Rinehart and Co., 1955), pp. 699–704.

tion, the widsom, nor the power to make or regulate rates for the purpose of
determining whether goods shall be bought or sold, manufactured, or consumed
in one section or locality .... "[8] Again, though, while the ICC has rarely forced
preferential regional rates into being, it has forced such preferences to *remain*
in being after they have become established.

Railroad Rates from the Pacific Northwest

A few studies of rate structures, particularly railway freight rate structures,
have attempted some appraisal of these structures in relation to the welfare and
needs of particular regions. For example, in a study of railroad rates from the
Pacific Northwest, Sampson considers the outbound rail rates on fourteen leading commodities in which the states of Oregon and Washington have large export
surpluses.[9] These are chiefly forest and agricultural products transported by
rail for long distances to markets concentrated geographically in the Great Lakes-
Northeast, the Southeast, Texas, and California. Rail service and especially rate
levels and structures, owing to the cooperation of carriers whose economic interests coincide with regional goals, were found to facilitate the wide distribution
of the region's exports and to be wholly satisfactory. The commodity rates as of
1961 were shown to embrace such features as a marked tapering of rate scales,
wide blankets or zones (lumber rates were blanketed from Chicago to New York),
holddowns on long-haul traffic in the postwar general rate increases, and some
rates that were less than fully compensatory.

It is interesting to note the findings with respect to rate-cost relationships
and their competitive implications. The data related to shipments from Western
(which includes Pacific Northwest) to Official Territory and their source was the
ICC revenue contribution calculations. On one group of four commodities (including aluminum bars, seeds, sugar, and wallboard), revenues more than covered
fully distributed costs. On a second group (lumber, plywood, wood pulp, and
building woodwork and millwork), revenues exceeded out-of-pocket costs but
did not cover fully distributed costs. These forest products meet strong competition in Official Territory from similar commodities produced in the South. Rates
on all of these products from Southern to Official Territory, interestingly
enough, were calculated to be well above fully distributed cost. On a third group
of five agricultural products, (frozen vegetables, potatoes, onions, apples, and
pears), revenues did not cover out-of-pocket costs. These comparisons, if they
accurately depict the situation, indicate that the rates from the Pacific Northwest
are indeed favorable on the whole to the region. Since rates on the agricultural
products here involved are probably relatively low in general, the Pacific North-

---

8. Lake Cargo Coal, 139 ICC 367, 391 (1928).

9. Roy J. Sampson, *Railroad Shipments and Rates from the Pacific Northwest*
(Eugene: University of Oregon, Bureau of Business Research, 1961).

west may obtain no undue advantage in the marketing of these commodities. With respect to forest products, however, the rate pattern could conceivably work to expand markets and output beyond that warranted by comparative advantage.

In his more general conclusions, Sampson asserts (but without documentation) that the type of transport system available to a region influences the level and the kind of economic activity. He sees the need for studies of freight rates in relation to other regional economies and of the effects of such services and restrictions as permissible routings, in-transit privileges, and diversions in transit. With greater knowledge of the effects of transport decisions, it may be possible, he suggests, "even to use transportation policy as an instrument in furthering our regional or national economic goals."[10]

South Pacific Coast Transcontinental Rates

In a study of transcontinental rate structures with special reference to California, Daggett and Carter disclose in detail the complexities of the eastbound and westbound rate structures and the competitive, geographical, and historical factors which have shaped them.[11] On the all-important commodity tariffs, extensive grouping or blanketing prevailed. A standard pattern of groupings of eastern origins was usually adopted for westbound manufacturers. On eastbound agricultural produce, fresh and processed, the groupings of eastern destinations were tailored to fit the demand and competitive features of specific exports. Practically all territory east of the Rockies was blanketed for wine and dried fruits and vegetables. And on citrus fruits the area roughly east of the Missouri and Mississippi Rivers was divided into three zones, the whole Northeast comprising a single zone. The citrus structure had the intended effects of enabling California shippers to meet the competition of Florida growers, of making diversions easier, and of placing interior distributors on a parity. Such incidental effects of zoning, particularly where zones are large, of encouraging circuitous routing and offsetting advantages of location were subordinated to the chief objective of facilitating the penetration of eastern markets.

This objective was sought by favorable adjustments in the level of rates as well. It was found that eastbound rates on major California exports were "generally low."[12] Most depressed were rates on canned goods, sugar, wine, citrus, and dried fruit. The question had been raised, it was noted, as to whether rates on

---

10. Sampson, op. cit., p. 62. See, also, Roy J. Sampson and Martin T. Farris, *Domestic Transportation: Practice, Theory and Policy* (Boston: Houghton Mifflin Co., 1966), where the authors consider the most appropriate freight rate policies for regions in various stages of development (pp. 212–217).

11. Stuart Daggett and John P. Carter, *The Structure of Transcontinental Railroad Rates* (Berkeley: University of California Press, 1947).

12. Ibid., pp. 126, 139.

some products actually covered out-of-pocket costs. Rates on imports into California, on the other hand, were found not "obviously favorable" to western consumers or manufacturers.[13]

The authors concluded that the transcontinental rate system was clearly advantageous to western agriculture. They reserved judgment in relation to the total economy, however, pending further study of the potentialities of western industry and agriculture, the industrial objectives of the Pacific Coast, and the most desirable relations with other regions.[14] In other words, they felt a rate structure favoring one sector of a region's economy could impede the development of a dynamic economy along the most promising lines.

Citrus Fruit Rates

The issue of the economic validity of the citrus rate structure was also joined in an analysis by Bigham and Roberts.[15] The typical relation of rates to a major common market (New York) from the three leading producing areas was reported as follows:[16]

	Rate per cwt.	Distance in miles	Revenue per ton-mile, cents
California	$1.68	3,073	1.093
Texas	1.49	2,171	1.373
Florida	1.19	1,188	2.003

With the rate structure shaped largely by the producer competition and not transport costs, rate-level adjustments over the years had been made in such a manner as to maintain more or less fixed differentials and thus permit each producing region to compete in the large eastern market. Although rates were higher, California could compete at prices about 20 percent higher than Florida oranges because of such factors as earlier seasonal entry into the market, more uniform quality, and more intensive advertising.

Emphasized by the authors were such pertinent considerations as the near noncompensatory level of the California rates, the discriminatory character of the western citrus blanket structure, and the costliness of diversions in transit. But the crucial factor in the argument was the finding that costs of production, including growing and marketing (excluding transport) costs, were lower in Florida than in California. Also, the elasticity of supply was greater in Florida. The depressed California rates discriminated against Florida and thereby destroyed

---

13. Ibid., p. 160.

14. Ibid., pp. 158–159, 161.

15. Truman C. Bigham and Merrill J. Roberts, *Citrus Fruit Rates: Development and Economic Appraisal* (Gainesville: University of Florida Press, 1950).

16. Ibid., pp. 85–88.

this comparative advantage. An uneconomic allocation of resources, chiefly of land, would be the consequence.

Regulation, it was observed, had been much less influential than competition in shaping the structure of citrus rates. The ICC had considered the Texas and California rates in only a few instances, and while Florida rates had been before it on many more occasions, the resulting modifications had not changed the basic pattern of rates. Although the ICC has refused to break up the long-established California blanket for fear of disrupting trade relations, it has accepted the blanketing scheme with reluctance. In declining to establish a similar blanket for Florida, it stated that it would not have been justified in setting up groupings as extensive as those on California citrus.

The adoption of mileage scales from all points of origin was recommended as a solution to the problem of limiting the force of carrier competition and preserving the advantages of location.

New England Freight Rates

The structure and level of freight rates, both rail and motor carrier, have been investigated in relation to New England's competitive position.[17] Regulatory rate decisions and railway rate policies have traditionally been of major concern to the region, two fairly recent examples being the prescription of the uniform classification and class-rate system and the elimination of the North Atlantic port differentials. Geographic location and the great importance of the manufacturing sector in New England's economy have made it peculiarly dependent on efficient transport service and satisfactory freight rates. Movements of raw materials and fuel into and finished goods out of New England are usually for longer distances than for competing producers located in the Middle Atlantic and East North Central states. Average railway hauls, for example, are longer than the national average.[18] Only in the case of raw materials indigenous to the region (pulpwood, lumber, and stone) or those imported from abroad (wool, rubber, hides, and sugar) do New England users have an advantage in freight

---

17. The Committee of New England of the National Planning Association, *The Economic State of New England* (New Haven: Yale University Press, 1954), Chapters 12 and 13. Chapter 12, entitled *Freight Rates and New England's Competitive Position*, was drafted by William H. Miernyk and was based largely on his *Railroad Transportation Charges to New England and Competing Shippers* (Staff Memorandum No. 3, June 1952, mimeographed). New England Governors' Committee on Public Transportation, *Public Transportation for New England*; No. 5, *Motor Freight Transport for New England* (Research report by Robert A. Nelson, October 1956); No. 9, *New England Highway and Rail Freight Rates* (Research reports by Robert A. Nelson, *New England Highway Freight Rates*, February 1957, and Martin L. Lindahl, *Railroad Freight Rates and New England Competitive Position*, May 1957). James R. Nelson, *Railroad Mergers and the Economy of New England* (Boston: The New England Economic Research Foundation, 1966).

18. James R. Nelson, op. cit., p. 93.

charges. Numerous rate comparisons have indicated unfavorable transport costs
on finished goods exports in relation to competing producers. An advantage in
transport costs has prevailed, however, on some manufactures moving to a limited
market to the west and south. In the case of highly specialized or differentiated
products in such fields as textiles, machinery, tools, electrical appliances, and
canned foodstuffs, markets were much more extensive than seemed warranted by
considering comparative advantage alone. The growth of rail shipments of manufactures to more distant markets, including the Pacific Coast, between 1950 and
1960, gave evidence of a comparative cost advantage on similar commodities
or a differentiation of product sufficient to command prices high enough to cover
the relatively high transport cost.[19]

There appeared to be no general discrimination in rail freight rates against
New England. Class rates were uniform and rough comparisons of commodity
rates indicated no marked disparities.[20] While inbound coal rates appeared to be
relatively high and rates on inward movements of agricultural and forest products
relatively low, a comparison of car-mile revenues on comparable hauls indicated
that New England shippers and users of manufactures have not suffered ratewise
in relation to the rest of the country.[21] This favorable showing in rates on manufactures, the largest category in New England's interregional traffic, reflected in
part the availability of special commodity rates, carload rates based on alternative minimum weights, and the westbound Canadian differential rates.[22] Westbound rates on manufactures as a whole, however, were found not to reflect the
dominant movement of empty cars in that direction. Neither regulation nor competition had achieved this result over the years.

Highway freight rates and related factors of cost, entry, and structure are of
singular importance because New England is more heavily dependent on highway
transport than the country as a whole. Notable features of the region's highway
transport have been the preponderance of short hauls and the substantially
higher charges per ton-mile for short than for long hauls. Among the factors accounting for the higher rates and costs on short hauls have been the (1) small
average load, (2) the large terminal costs per vehicle-mile, (3) the absence of railway competition. The key factor of small average loads has been attributed to
inordinate service competition, which requires more vehicles and more frequent
service, encouraged in part by the suppression of rate competition under ICC

19. Ibid., pp. 118–121.

20. Lindahl, op. cit., p. 77

21. James R. Nelson, op. cit., pp. 97, 108, 125.

22. For many years a small freight rate differential has been provided for certain westbound movements from New England routed over Canadian carriers, apparently on the
theory that the ICC had no jurisdiction and that the routings were a long way around and
slower, hence should get a favored rate. Indeed since the Canadian roads have improved their
service considerably, such "out-of-the-way" service may presently be superior, negating the
latter argument. One might apply the same arguments to eastbound movements as well, but
no differential has been introduced.

Motor Rate Bureau regulation. Entry controls may also have made for inflexibility of route patterns and restrictions on the expansion of the more efficient carriers. Such factors as more severe climatic conditions and inadequate highways, factors often cited by the carriers, have been minimized as explanations for higher than nationwide operating costs and rates in the region.

As for whether the competitive position of the New England region was adversely affected by highway freight rates, the most authoritative view (in 1957) was that "in general New England shippers do not suffer competitive disadvantages insofar as highway carrier rates are concerned."[23] This was found to be true for class rates as well as commodity rates. Class rates on traffic between New England and other territories beyond eastern New York were based not on the region's unique cost-based system but on the rail rates applicable in other territories. Rate comparisons in specific situations indicated that favorable commodity rates had also been accorded New England shippers who were competitive with shippers outside of the region. One reservation to the generally favorable picture was that more traffic moved on class rates within the region, as opposed to commodity rates, than in other territories.

Concern has been expressed over the ICC's proclivity to prescribe distance scales for general application based on average operating costs of carrier groups. While such rate systems tended to eliminate some types of discrimination, to stabilize rates, and to protect earnings, they also tended to restrict rate-making freedom on the part of individual carriers. Carriers were limited in their discretion to quote special commodity rates based on lower costs stemming from such factors as greater volume of movement or better terrain. New England had benefited from such highway rates, and rail rates too, in interregional competition and any disposition to cancel commodity rates or to prevent their introduction would work to the injury of the region.

Summary

It seems apparent that rate structures and levels somewhat influence the pattern of regional development. The individual carriers, on the whole, have adjusted freight rates so as best to meet the economic needs of the localities and regions which they serve. This has been true of regions such as the Pacific Coast where the economies have been closely tied to long-haul rail transport. Competition in its various manifestations has probably influenced freight rates to a greater degree than regulation. Regulatory authorities have been disposed to accept and perpetuate rate situations that were solidified by competitive forces prior to or even since the inception of control. In so doing, they probably have sanctioned rate levels and relationships which have distorted the relative advantages of com-

---

23. Robert A. Nelson, op. cit., p. 53.

peting regions. But regulation has had a positive impact also in removing some discriminatory barriers which might have impeded regional growth. The trends toward distance scales and cost of service pricing have tended to reduce spatial discrimination and to insure the advantage of location. But rate structures once established under regulatory authority tend to be rigid and inflexible and are slow to change in conformity with changing technology and competitive forces. Greater freedom on the part of individual modes and carriers to adjust rates and services to meet new conditions and special situations would contribute to the flexibility of the system.

Suggestions for Improvement of Current Practices and Regulation in the Regional Context

There are several areas in which improvements in the content and efficiency of regulation could contribute to regional development.

Regulatory Lag

A long-standing problem has been the time-consuming nature, cumbersomeness, and costliness of the regulatory process. Regulated carriers, as a result, have been handicapped in adjusting rates to take advantage of new technological or competitive opportunities. In talking about the slowness of response to technological change, the Council of Economic Advisers cited the case of the "Big John" freight car service.[24] Originally announced in June 1961, it was not until September 1965 and after protracted proceedings in the ICC and the courts that the reduced rates were finally approved. Consumer savings from the 60 percent reduction in rates and the resulting expansion of the livestock and grain industries in the Southern Railway region were substantial. Remarked the Council: "No economy can be fully efficient if it takes four years to determine pricing for such innovations." While the difficult substantive issue of the place of cost-oriented rates in intermodal competition was the deterrent in this case, this kind of experience has not been unusual in major rate and merger cases.

Relaxation of Controls

Reducing formal regulation and placing greater reliance upon competition for control of rates and service and the allocation of transportation resources would be a desirable shift in policy.[25] Such deregulation should embrace freer

24. Council of Economic Advisers, *Annual Report* (1966), p. 129.

25. See Merton J. Peck, "Competitive Policy for Transportation;" in Almarin Phillips, ed. *Perspectives on Antitrust Policy* (Princeton: Princeton University Press, 1965).

entry into highway and water transportation and, at a minimum, lifting minimum rate regulation on traffic in bulk and agricultural commodities. Such relaxation of rate control on commodities subject to heavy nonregulated competition, coupled with an appropriate system of user charges, would equalize competitive opportunity and should result in lower rates and a modest shift in traffic to the railroads. Under this minimal program, the ICC would retain control over all maximum rates and over all forms of discrimination, thus assuring continued protection to regions that might otherwise suffer because of the unevenness of competition.

Intermodal Rate Policy

Even if minimum rate control on bulk and agricultural products were to be eliminated, there would still remain for regulatory disposition the problem of appropriate standards for minimum rates on manufactures and miscellaneous traffic. It is on this class of traffic that the greatest opportunities for competitive rate reductions exist, owing to the higher average mark-up over long-run out-of-pocket rail costs than on bulk and agricultural products. A significant volume of total rail traffic moves at rates yielding revenues ranging from 170 to 500 percent and over of out-of-pocket costs.[26] Although the ratios of revenues to out-of-pocket costs have declined in recent years, several remaining possibilities for competitive rate reductions are quite apparent.

While the railways have made modest reductions in rates on a wide range of commodities and very deep cuts in a few cases, they have not met with unqualified success in having their proposals approved by the ICC.[27] One deterrent has been the attachment of the ICC to full-cost criteria in assessing the validity of rate reductions in several *important* cases — even though in the great majority of intermodal rate cases the cost evidence has related to out-of-pocket costs rather than to fully distributed costs.[28] In general, better resource allocation would be achieved with the acceptance of long-run marginal cost or the Commission's near equivalent of long-run out-of-pocket[29] as the appropriate minimum standard for pricing. Fixed costs would have to be met, unless the carriers were subsidized, with rates on some traffic at levels above marginal cost where demand elasticities permit under current competitive conditions. Some contribution to overhead could also be made by raising rates on the substantial volume of traffic which now moves at rates below the ICC's measure of out-of-pocket costs. A continuation of the trend in the direction of cost-oriented rates would reduce the marked

26. Merrill J. Roberts, "Transport Costs, Pricing and Regulation," in Universities — National Bureau Committee for Economic Research, *Transportation Economics* (New York: National Bureau of Economic Research, 1965), pp. 30–32.

27. Ibid., pp. 20–26.

28. Ibid., pp. 18–20.

29. George Wilson, "The Effect of Rate Regulation on Resource Allocation in Transportation," *American Economic Review*, Vol. LIV, No. 3 (May 1964), p. 161.

degree of rate discrimination which still exists and any adverse effects stemming therefrom on resource allocation in the nontransport sector of the economy. Lower rates on manufactures would be of particular benefit to manufacturing enterprises long-established at substantial distances from their markets and thus might tend to slow up the trend toward decentralization of manufacturing activity.[30]

Rate Policy as a Device for Promoting Development of Depressed Areas

The manipulation of freight rates to encourage development in depressed areas has sometimes been suggested. Transport companies, the railways in particular, have found their prosperity or lack of it bound to the welfare of the regions which they serve and have made rate adjustments which would promote a wide geographic distribution of commodities produced in their service areas. Parenthetically, one of the weaknesses of the New England railways has been their small control over long-haul competitive rates.

Notable examples of the setting of favorable rates for regional development purposes have been the large blankets and relatively low rates on agricultural and forest products from the Pacific Coast to Eastern markets. This may be unobjectionable if the rates cover marginal costs, but where they do not, such rates clearly lead to an uneconomic allocation of resources both in the transport and in the nontransport sectors of the economy. Depressed rates on some of these commodities may actually be contributing to the difficulties encountered by such problem areas as Appalachia and the Upper Great Lakes in realizing their growth potentialities. There is the possibility also that rate structures once established to achieve specific development goals will retard later potential development in other sectors of the regional economy with shifts in demand or other changed conditions. A rate structure favorable to Pacific Coast agriculture, for example, may impede the growth of manufacturing in the region unless the carriers can afford favorable rate adjustments on industrial raw materials and finished manufactures.

So far as regulation is concerned, it has already been noted that the ICC has rarely asserted its power in a positive manner to influence the location of industry. The ICC will not compel carriers to make rate reductions in order to offset locational disadvantages. Perhaps indirectly, by taking into account the effects of rates on the movement of traffic or the injunction of the Hoch-Smith Resolution to recognize economic conditions in industry or agriculture, rates have been prescribed·in recognition of producer competition. On both theoretical

---

30. Benjamin Chinitz, *Freight and the Metropolis* (Cambridge: Harvard University Press, 1960), pp. 172–174.

and practical grounds, however, the policy of prescribing rates on cost and distance factors is to be preferred.

All this is not to say that freight rates and services on all modes of transport may not be investigated to advantage to see whether or not more favorable adjustments may be warranted. West Virginia producers of wood products, for example, were able to obtain commodity and incentive rates comparable to those from other producing regions in the postwar period.[31] In addition to rates, investigations of service features such as routing restrictions, stopovers for processing, diversions in transit, coordination of modes, and the like may be fruitful in uncovering ways to advance the interests of regional producers within the context of regulation.

----

31. Thomas C. Campbell, *Freight Rates of West Virginia Wood Products* (West Virginia Economic Development Series, West Virginia University, 1965), pp. 19–23.

7 Urban Transportation as a Factor in Metropolitan Growth

The past several decades have seen a trend toward regionalization of production within the American economy. This trend has not, however, in any sense diminished the importance of cities as population and production centers. The trend towards decentralization, and the general growth of the economy, have on the contrary, been manifested in the growth of both old and new urban areas. Thus to a great extent regional development is the development of urban centers.

State of the Art

When agglomeration factors enter the locational calculus, cities are seen as competitors offering, among other things, a transportation system to a limited number of firms seeking locations. The leverage of urban transportation in attracting industry clearly depends upon the importance of urban transportation in the locational decisions of firms. Unfortunately, very little is known about this. Numerous studies have documented the movement of industry to particular urban freeways. But they have generally failed to show that transport investments induced industry to move *to* the metropolitan region rather than simply relocating *within* the region.

The state of the art is currently not sufficiently advanced to predict the locational attraction of urban transportation. All else equal, a city with a good transportation system would certainly be more desirable than one with a poor transportation system. When transportation is generally poor, the improvement of transportation facilities may prove to be very strategic. The early growth of the port cities is a case in point. But when transportation is generally good and product values per unit weight are increasing, making transport even better may have little, if any, effect. Consider for example, a firm that must choose a location in either of two cities, and suppose that the firm plans to ship its product an average of 500 miles in either case. If the shipment from the first city costs 1¢ ton-mile and from the second 2¢ / ton-mile, and the production costs of the product are $990/ton, the firm would save only one-half of 1 percent on the delivered cost by locating in the first city. If all else were equal it would do so. But it is clear that only a small favorable departure from the "all else equal" condition would be necessary for the city with the higher transportation cost to be chosen.

In general, the growth of metropolitan regions has obviously placed demands on urban transportation systems, both in terms of capacity and of the spatial

83

distribution of service. From a narrow point of view, transportation investments in response to these demands can be considered as expenditures on a capital good to be used in the production process. Like any other investment, transportation investments might be expected to cover their costs, and, subject to appropriate budget constraints and discount rates, those transport projects which maximize benefits should be built. To the extent that investments which can recover their costs are not undertaken, the production process is less efficient than it might be and, in this sense, growth is hampered.

Transportation and Development of Suburban Areas

Industry in the United States initially centralized in urban areas to take advantage of the economies of large scale production. It located in cities first because of natural transportation advantages and later because of localization and urbanization economies. As cities have grown, however, congestion within them has increased and the supply of undeveloped land greatly decreased. Agglomeration economies continue to draw activity to metropolitan regions, but the various sorts of congestion encountered in the central city and the development of more space-intensive production techniques have tended to push industry to suburban fringes.

Similarly, the development of trucking, pipelines, and piggybacking have made access or proximity to centrally located rail sidings and marshalling yards and port facilities less important then they once were. With the increasing importance of regional industries and of industries producing high-value goods with low transport requirements, a relatively lower percentage of total industrial activity now needs access to the long-haul line-haul economies of rail and water transport. As a consequence, suburban land that is served only by highways (i.e., without direct access to rail or water) can now be a quite suitable location for much industrial activity. The net result has been an emerging pattern of geographical specialization within metropolitan regions, with headquarters, service and control activity generally located in the core, and new industrial plants increasingly distributed about the urban fringe.

Residential activity has followed industrial movements to some extent, but suburban living is also undoubtedly desired partly for the amenities it offers. Suburban living and the automobile are complementary goods which constitute a "bundle" of final demand. The general desire for suburban living and automobiles provides a massive reinforcement of the trend towards geographical specialization within the metropolitan region and, particularly, the availability of more job opportunities in suburban locations. The desire of consumers for private automobiles can also influence the choice among modes for freight shipments. Highways strictly for trucking, for example, might not be economical. But the ability of the highway to serve both the final demand for auto travel and the derived demands for freight, lowers the average cost of shipping freight by high-ways.

Modal Implications of Suburbanization

The preponderance of evidence strongly points to a continued decline of industrial and perhaps residential densities within central cities and to a perpetuation of recent levels of suburban industrial and residential densities in areas yet to be developed. It also seems reasonable to expect more industrial and business activities to be clustered at several points within a metropolitan region. This implies that different parts of the region may tend to transact day-to-day working and living routines as somewhat more self-contained and independent units. It is also becoming increasingly clear that the central cores of our older and larger metropolitan regions will continue to become more specialized, serving mainly as centers for such activities as banks, law firms, and the headquarters of large businesses.

These trends, if they continue, will diminish the magnitude of one large part of the urban transportation problem. Any specialization of activity and residential characteristics between suburbs and central cities should decrease travel along the more congested corridors radiating from the downtown core. The transportation needs for this pattern of urban development are clearly different from the high volume radial concentrations of transport service that are now generally observed.

In particular, public transportation should be highly flexible and mobile if it is to serve these new demands as they evolve. The system should be able to serve numerous origins and destinations and be able to accomodate many local enroute stops conveniently. The system must also be capable of adapting to the schedules, privacy, and comfort requirements of individual passengers, and if privacy is a primary requirement, no existing public mode is likely to be a strong competitor to the automobile. In general, dynamic considerations are important. A good system should be able to adapt readily to technological change and to change route structure continually to accomodate shifts in the patterns of industrial, business, and residential activity.

The automobile as it is known now meets these requirements. An equally satisfactory alternative, however, might be based on various types of transit or jitney bus services, that can provide door-to-door services nearly competitive with automobiles. Perhaps automated dispatching would facilitate the provision of such services. More glamorous technologies capable of operating both on dense, high-speed automated line-haul facilities and on city streets, might be reasonable alternatives some years from now.

With increasing incomes consumers tend to substitute private automobiles for public transportation. As incomes are expected to continue rising, this clearly implies at least a relative and probably an absolute decrease in demand for transit service. But even after the effects of increased income are taken into account, there has been a shift in consumer preferences from public transit to the private automobile.[1] None of this is very surprising. It only says that for most people in most situations the automobile travel "package" even with "vehicle congestion" and higher costs, seems more desirable than that of transit service, with its "people congestion," schedule and route inflexibility, and low cost. In general, increases in real income and changes in consumers' tastes have placed and will continue to place transit at an even greater disadvantage, all else equal.

Urban transportation policy decisions can also play an important negative role in metropolitan development by diverting funds from more productive investments. The cost-benefit aspect of transportation systems often *seems* to receive considerable attention. But the results of many decisions, it should be noted and emphasized, justify even more intensive analysis. Programs have often been sold to the public without sound economic analysis, and the tremendous initial and continuing costs of the resulting mistakes will probably, in time, dampen the development of several metropolitan regions.

These uneconomical ventures can take many forms. The net effect, however, is always the same: a commitment of resources that could have been used to better advantage on some other project. There is reason to think, for example, that many rural parts of the Interstate Highway System are uneconomical by virtually any measure.[2] At the other extreme, extensions of commuter service and rail rapid transit lines are very frequently much more costly than their benefits warrant, and often such benefits as they do provide accrue to the higher income segments of the region's population.[3] Waste is also often caused in urban highway programs by unreasonable and uneconomic safety and service standards, and by demanding too great a reduction in congestion.

Public decision makers have frequently been led to believe that sufficient transit usage will somehow materialize to take advantage of the scale economies of fixed, high capacity systems. This would imply, if it were true, that the massive program costs of transit are justified by their potentially very low average costs. However, both prewar and postwar experience has repeatedly documented that the potential scale economies of high capacity transit systems will seldom, if

---

1. See Walter Y. Oi and Paul W. Shuldiner, *An Analysis of Urban Travel Demands* (Evanston: Northwestern University Press for the Transportation Center at Northwestern, 1962).

2. For a very thorough analysis, see Ann Friedlaender, *The Interstate Highway System* (Amsterdam: North-Holland, 1965).

3. For a specific example, see David McNicol, "Some Income Transfers Associated with Extensions of Rail Rapid Transit Service to the Outer Suburbs of the Boston Metropolitan Region." Honors Thesis, Harvard University, April, 1966, and Martin Wohl, "Users of Urban Transportation Services and Their Income Circumstances," *Traffic Quarterly*, Vol. 24, No. 1 (January 1970).

ever, be realized in modern day urban American, because of insufficient demand. Recent trends toward suburbanization of industry and residences hold little hope of greatly altering this situation. And when sufficient demand is not forthcoming, the actual unit costs of providing transit service are not only higher than anticipated, but often higher than those of reasonable alternative systems.

It should also be noted that the usual cost studies and cost comparisons are generally improper and misleading. Most of them, for example, involve comparisons between transport systems with very different service conditions. They also frequently make comparisons based on the capacity of alternative systems, rather than on expected or actual usage. For example, it is common to compare the per track costs for a rapid transit line with a capacity of, say, 40,000 passengers an hour, with the per lane costs of a highway with a capacity of, say, 3,000 passengers in automobiles an hour. Such a comparison would indicate that there are substantial economies to be gained from substituting rapid transit facilities for highways. But such naive comparisons are clearly of little value as they ignore the differences in service levels as well as peak-to-off-peak demand differentials for the two types of systems. Furthermore, such comparisons ignore the fact that 30,000 per hour passenger volumes (or more) can easily be achieved for a highway lane if committed to bus use only.

The comparative cost characteristics of different urban transportation technologies have been analyzed elsewhere.[4] The systems studied were designed to operate at speeds, schedule frequencies, and so on, such that travelers would be "indifferent" to the various modes except for cost differences. These analyses indicated that for peak hour corridor volumes much below 7,000–8,000 passengers, no existing system can offer strong competition to the automobile, supplemented by the bus for public transit needs, either on a cost or on a service basis. Only about 15 urban centers in the United States have higher volumes today. These cost studies also showed that, for peak-hour corridor volumes of less than about 15,000 to 20,000 passengers, rail rapid transit service coupled with downtown subways and park-and-ride residential service is usually more costly, all things considered, than other forms of public transport. It should be noted that only five U.S. cities have peak hour corridor volumes above 20,000. Four of these cities already have large scale transit systems, and the fifth is now building one.

It was found that in most cases, including even the largest and densest American cities, bus service is not only cost competitive with rail, but also superior in certain service aspects. Properly designed bus services, for example, would often require fewer passenger transfers and less waiting time than rail technologies.

In summary, the evidence points to the desire of the traveling public for more flexible and mobile systems and for higher levels of service, whether auto

---

4. See John R. Meyer, John Kain and Martin Wohl, *The Urban Transportation Problem* (Cambridge: Harvard University Press, 1965), Part III, for a report of the study findings.

or transit. Except for cities with sunk costs in existing rapid transit systems, there appears to be little hope of transit competing with the automobile other than by offering at a competitive cost a service package at least as good as that of the automobile. It is also clear that more concern must be given to the development of more adaptable and shorter-life transit systems. The rapidly changing social, economic and technological environment make this a matter of fundamental importance, and makes the value of fixed transit systems even more doubtful. The entire automobile fleet turns over, on the average, once every eleven to twelve years. It is evident from this alone that an automobile system can take advantage of techological and social change much more rapidly than can a rail system, whose routes are fixed and whose equipment is designed conventionally for an economic life of between 30 to 40 years.

Interregional Aspects

In addition to its place within the city, urban transportation operates as the primary link between the intra- and interregional transportation systems. In this sense, the urban transportation system functions as a switchboard. The points of connection — terminals, exchanges, feeder links, etc. — are generally called the interface.

The extent and character of interregional movement seems to be closely related to the interface between inter- and intra-regional transportation systems, both for business and social recreational movements. The urban transportation system operates as a network to connect a market that warrants special service (such as intercity express transportation). It thus performs services for locations within the region that are not in the immediate urban areas. Studies, however, have shown that the business sector is often affected by the delay and inconvenience of inter-modal transfers, slow intraregional movement, and by centralized inter-city terminals. The social-recreational sector is probably more influenced by the "logistical" problem of inter-modal transfers, and by the effort involved in making the overall trip including the cost.

The changing structure of the production process, plant locations, and mobility of labor, together with changes in the relative costs of labor and capital, all require a transportation system which will permit more scheduling reliability and flexibility, and which will minimize the interface problems between inter- and intraregional modal links. This clearly emphasizes the importance of standardized containers and the importance of continued development of sophisticated operating control systems.

These features suggest some fairly dominant patterns for future interregional transport systems. The automobile will continue to dominate interregional social-recreational movements for many years to come. As incomes rise, however, combination road-rail systems and automated intercity highways are reasonable technological possibilities, at least within high density corridors such as that between Boston and Washington. It also seems likely that air transportation will play an increasingly important role in long-distance passenger movements. Of course, as technologies such as automated highways develop, it is possible, if not likely, that they could cause some shift away from shorter hauls by air. Within the near future, however, V/STOL aircraft and multiple V/STOL airports, each offering high frequency air service, may offset any tendency for short haul air traffic to decline.

Summary and Conclusions

The central issues of this study have been: Can transportation investments significantly stimulate regional development in the United States? Further, if transportation can help, what can it do, how much can it do, and at what cost can a transport-based development strategy be carried out?

To approach these questions, it is necessary to distinguish clearly between the active and passive roles of transportation in development. A region which is growing will almost certainly require additional transportation facilities. Failure to provide the necessary increases in the capacity of the transportation system will create bottlenecks and may eventually retard the region's growth. In this case transportation plays a purely negative and passive role. In other cases, transportation investments may cause regional growth, or operationally, transportation may create its own demand by stimulating the location of industrial activity.

The active role of transportation can be considered in terms of regional economics, international trade theory and location theory. In recent years these fields have been integrated into what can reasonably be called a preliminary theory of what transportation can do to stimulate regional development. The conclusion is that, *in theory,* transportation investment will sometimes cause regional growth.

The theory assumes that the various regions will be treated unequally. Transportation investment can be used to give a particular region an advantage in transportation, relative to other regions. The theory shows that this relative transport advantage will lead to regional growth. However, this mechanism clearly will not operate if the transport systems of all regions are improved. Transportation investments may also be helpful in a slightly different case. If a region has a good growth potential because of raw materials, skilled labor, etc., but because of historical or political accident has a poor transportation system, transport investment in that region may promote its growth.

While correct in theory, two major factors throw considerable doubt on the relevance of these considerations to current conditions in the United States:

1. The transportation system in the United States is already very highly developed. Any regional transportation system can be only a small addition to an already vast and efficient network and, therefore, its effects are likely to be small.

2. The production process is changing. Products are becoming more highly fabricated, raw materials are less important, and production is becoming more divisible. All of these changes imply a relatively decreasing importance for transportation in the locational decisions of firms.

It is also important to recognize that industry in the United States is beginning to "regionalize" for reasons which are only partly related to transportation.

91

The theory has generally assumed that each industry will tend to concentrate at one or a few locations, and has therefore focused on interregional links. The idea was that a region must grow by increasing its exports to other regions. The trends toward industrial regionalization imply that a region can grow by attracting regional industry and this shifts the focus toward intraregional transportation.

Another recent trend of some importance is the emergence of what are called "footloose" industries. These industries do not appear to place as much emphasis on the traditional locational considerations, such as the availability of raw materials, labor supply, market size and transportation costs. They seem, rather, to locate on the basis of what we can call amenity factors such as climate or educational resources provided by major universities.

These factors suggest that transportation investment generally will not be a very significant stimulus to further regional growth in the United States. The conclusion cannot be entirely negative, however. In order to capitalize on the trend toward regionalization of industry, for example, a region must have a good intraregional transportation system. This clearly suggests emphasis on regional highways. Similarly, the footloose industries often require fast, effective long-haul passenger transport. Regions hoping to attract such industries must, therefore, look carefully at their air transport systems.

Little need be said about the theory of the passive role of transportation. It is obvious that, if desired development is being retarded by a lack of transport capacity, transport investments should be made. The problem in this case is primarily one of estimating demand, and providing a transport sector suited to meeting the demands placed on it.

Regionalization of industry may also place new demands on the transport sector, besides the need for intraregional travel. Industries are moving about the country toward a more even regional distribution, but a trend also continues of locating in and around urban areas. The movement of industry and population to the suburbs leaving management, control, and service activities in the central city, is producing a new pattern of travel in metropolitan areas. This new pattern of travel seems generally to require a more flexible and ubiquitous system than that offered by fixed route public mass transit systems.

In conclusion, it is important to realize that the management of the transportation system poses problems which can affect regional development. The regulation of transportation, in particular, can by omission or commission aid or retard development. Further, transportation systems, like other capital goods, continuously wear out and must be replaced, and must also keep pace with growth. The very rapid rate of technological advance in the United States makes it imperative that, in replacing and expanding the transportation system, attention be paid both to emerging potentials and the rate of change of technology. What is good today may be out of date tomorrow, and a region burdened with debts still due on an outmoded transport system may be little aided in its growth ambitions.

Appendix: Mathematical Transportation Models

The so-called linear programming transportation problem was first presented by F. L. Hitchcock[1] in 1941. In its original form, the model was intended to solve the transportation problem at the industry level. Given the supplies and demands at every possible production and consumption location, and a fixed transportation cost between every pair of locations, the model purports to find the pattern of distribution which minimizes this total transportation cost while satisfying all the demands of consumption locations exactly without exceeding the supplies of production locations. Hitchcock showed that this implied a particular type of linear program and that there is a simple algorithm for solving the problem rather than by using the general linear programming simplex method. Koopmans[2] (1949) introduced this problem to economics. Enke[3] (1951) demonstrated that interregional trade problems for given production and transportation conditions can be solved by electric analogue.

Samuelson [4] (1952) showed that the general interregional equilibrium problem can be solved more generally with the use of linear programming. The technique was applied to the livestock feed industry by Fox[5] (1953) and to the coal industry by Henderson (1958)[6]

The solution of an interregional linear programming problem implies the common sense implication that a region should supply to another region as long as the cost of direct shipment is equal to or below the cost of shipping to the region indirectly (the opportunity cost). A significant by-product of this method is that the solution gives not only the optimal pattern of distribution but also relative locational advantages among supply locations and among demand locations. Consequently, if the costs of improving transportation links are known, the technique can be used for identifying priorities among alternative programs. The relative advantage of a production location is in the traditional sense the location rent. The link between the locational rent theory and the solution by

---

1. F. L. Hitchcock, "The Distribution of a Product from Several Sources of Numerous Localities," *Journal of Mathematics and Physics*, Vol. 20 (1941).

2. Tjalling C. Koopmans, "Optimum Utilization of the Transportation System," *Econometrica*, Vol. 17, Supplement (July, 1949).

3. Stephen Enke, "Equilibrium Among Spatially Separated Markets: Solution by Electric Analogue," *Econometrica*, Vol. 19, No. 1 (January, 1951).

4. Paul Samuelson, "Spatial Price Equilibrium and Linear Programming," *American Economic Review*, Vol. 42, No. 3 (June, 1952).

5. K. A. Fox, "A Spatial Equilibrium Model of the Livestock-Feed Economy in the United States," *Econometrica*, Vol. 21, No. 4 (October, 1953).

6. James M. Henderson, *The Efficiency of the Coal Industry* (Cambridge: Harvard University Press, 1958).

the linear programming transportation solution is discussed by Stevens (1961)[7]

The linear programming formulation of interregional equilibrium was presented by Isard (1958)[8], Lefeber (1958)[9], and Stevens (1958)[10], while extension of the traditional general equilibrium analysis to multiregional economy were made concurrently by Isard (1957) and Isard and Ostroff (1957).[11] Interregional linear programming models have been developed with special reference to underdeveloped countries by Harwitz (1965)[12] and to regions of the United States by Harwitz and Hurter (1964).[13]

The general interregional models are conceptually superior to partial equilibrium analysis of the traditional location theory, and add to our understanding of the exchange mechanism in spatially extended economies. The role of transportation to the economy as a whole, and to a particular region can be determined with the use of the models. However, they have practical drawbacks in that the solution cannot be determined unless the model is implemented with empirical data. The model is so complex that its empirical implementation is time-consuming and very costly. Furthermore, these models are not entirely satisfactory because of their rigid assumptions on the forms of the production functions, production technology, and final demands.

---

7. Benjamin H. Stevens, "Linear Programming and Location Rent," *Journal of Regional Science*, Vol. 3, No. 2, (Winter, 1961).

8. Walter Isard, "Interregional Programming: An Elementary Presentation and a General Model," *Journal of Regional Science*, Vol. 1, No. 1 (Summer, 1958).

9. Louis Lefeber, *Allocation in Space* (Amsterdam: North-Holland, 1958).

10. Benjamin Stevens, "An Interregional Linear Programming Model," *Journal of Regional Science*, Vol. 1, No. 1 (Summer, 1958).

11. Walter Isard and David Ostroff, "The Existence of a Competitive Interregional Equilibrium," *Papers and Proceedings of the Regional Science Association*, Vol. 4 (1958).

12. Mitchell Harwitz, "Regional Development Policy," in Gary Fromm, ed., *Transportation Investment and Economic Development* (Washington: The Brookings Institution, Transport Research Program, 1965).

13. Harwitz and Hurter, op. cit. This model is formally very similar to the Harwitz model cited above, but its application is somewhat different.

Bibliography

This is not a complete nor a comprehensive bibliography of all materials which bear on the role of transportation in regional economic development, but rather a minimum set of titles which adequately covers major aspects of the topic. A high degree of selectivity was exercised in choosing the titles to be included. The major criterion was relevance to the role of transportation in *development*.

Detailed bibliographies are included in several of the works listed below. The listings following each chapter of Isard's *Methods of Regional Analysis* (I. C. 11) offer a very complete survey of the literature. *Review of Techniques of Regional Analysis* (I. C. 23) by the Stanford Research Institute includes a good bibliography on Regional Science, as does John Meyer's "Regional Economics: A Survey," (I. C. 18). The most important sources in urban transportation are noted in Meyer, Kain, and Wohl, *The Urban Transportation Problem*, (I. E. 12). *Sources of Information in Transportation* published by Northwestern University Press for the Transportation Center at Northwestern is the most complete and easily used single bibliography. *Current Literature in Traffic and Transportation*, also published by the Transportation Center, offers good coverage of the trade journals and picks up major books in transportation. The more technical literature is surveyed annually in *Transportation Research*, published by the Transportation Association of America.[1]

There is no single book, or even a group of four or five books, which adequately treats the role of transportation in regional development. The key references have, however, been identified and marked with an asterisk. In addition, the books listed below, all of which are collections of articles, are useful for a general survey of current issues in the field.

Friedman, John and William Alonso. *Regional Development and Planning: A Reader*. Cambridge: M.I.T. Press, 1964.

Fromm, Gary, ed. *Transport Investment and Economic Development*. Washington: The Brookings Institution Transport Research Program, 1965.

National Academy of Sciences - National Research Council. *Conference on Transportation Research*. NAS-NRC publication 840. Washington: NAS-NRC, 1960.

_____. *Transportation Design Considerations*. NAS-NRC publication 841. Washington: NAS-NRC, 1961.

---

1. Transportation Association of America, 1101 17th Street, N.W., Washington, D. C.

____. *U. S. Transportation Resources, Performance, and Problems.* NAS-NRC publication 841–S. Washington: NAS-NRC, 1961.

Universities - National Bureau Committee for Economic Research. *Transportation Economics.* A conference of the Universities - National Bureau Committee for Economic Research. New York: National Bureau of Economic Research, 1965.

I. Theory and Related Empirical Studies

A. Geography and Social Physics

1. Baskin, Carlisle, W. *A Critique and Translation of Water Christaller's Die Zentralen Ort in Suddeutschland.* Charlottesville: University of Virginia, 1957. (Doctoral Dissertation). (German ed. Jena: Gustav Fisher, 1933).

   Christaller's work is the foundation of central place theory.

*2. Berry, Brian. *Interregional Flow Forecasting Model: A General Field Theory.* Chicago: University of Chicago, Department of Geography, 1966.

   This study presents a statistically constructed spatial equilibrium model in which commodity flows and areal attributes, including linkage characteristics, are mutually correlated.

3. Carrothers, G. A. P. "An Historical Review of the Gravity and Potential Concepts of Human Interaction." *Journal of the American Institute of Planners,* Vol. 22, No. 2 (Spring, 1956).

   This article traces the origins of the concept to an anlogy with Newton's physics. A good bibliography is included.

4. Gottman, Jean. *Megalopolis: The Urbanized Northeastern Seaboard of the United States.* New York: The Twentieth Century Fund, 1961.

   Chapter 12 contains a description of general trends of transportation in the United States.

5. Logan, Richard F. "The Shifting Patterns of Travel in the Southwestern Deserts." *Annals of the American Association of Geographers,* Vol. 45 (1955).

   This article describes the impact of rail and highway on activity in the Mojave Desert.

6. Thoman, Richard S. *The Geography of Economic Activity.* New York: McGraw-Hill, 1962.

This book is a well rounded introduction to economic geography for non- and semi-professionals.

*7. Ullman, Edward L. "Amenities as a Factor in Regional Growth." *Geographical Review*, Vol. 49 (1954).

The author speculates that amenity factors such as climate are increasingly important as determinants of regional growth and migration.

8. ____. "Regional Development and the Geography of Concentration." *Papers and Proceedings of the Regional Science Association*, Vol. 4 (1958).

This article is an empirical analysis of U. S. geography which concludes that initial locational advantages at crucial stages of development lead eventually to massive localization.

B. International Trade

1. Kindelberger, Charles P. *International Economics*. Homewood, Ill.: Richard D. Irwin, 1958 (revised ed.).

This book is a standard text on international trade. For the effect of transport costs on trade see pp. 142–147.

*2. Ohlin, Bertil. *Interregional and International Trade*. Cambridge: Harvard University Press, 1933. (3rd printing, 1957).

The author argues that the foundations of interregional trade theory are based on differentials in resource endowments and transfer costs.

C. Location Theory and Regional Economics

1. Alonso, William. *Location and Land Use*. Cambridge: Harvard University Press, 1964.

An equilibrium model of urban land use is presented within the framework of neoclassical economics and traditional location theory. For the impact of transportation see in particular pp. 130–142 (City Shapes).

2. ____. "Location Theory." In John Friedman and William Alonso, eds. *Regional Development and Planning: A Reader*. Cambridge: The M. I. T. Press, 1964.

This is a good introduction to the theory of the location of a firm.

3. ____. "A Reformulation of Classical Location Theory and its Relation to

Rent Theory" in Morgan D. Thomas, ed. *Papers, the St. Louis Meeting, November 1966. Vol. 19* Regional Science Association, 1967.

4. Barloon, Marvin J. "The Interrelationship of the Changing Structure of American Transportation and Changes in Industrial Location." *Land Economics*, Vol. XLI, No. 2 (May, 1965).

    This article discusses the impact of changing production processes on location decisions of firms.

5. Chinitz, Benjamin. "Contrasts in Agglomeration: New York and Pittsburgh." *American Economic Review*, Vol. 51, No. 3 (May, 1961).

    The author criticizes current regional analysis and emphasizes the supply side – factors such as quality of management, labor, etc., which influence production costs.

6. Fuchs, V. R. "The Determinants of the Redistribution of Manufacturing in the United States Since 1929." *Review of Economics and Statistics*, Vol. 44, No. 2 (May, 1962).

    The author argues that most important industrial redistributions occurred in labor- or resource-oriented industries.

7. Hill, Donald M., "A Growth Allocation Model for the Boston Region," *Journal of the American Institute of Planners*, Vol. 31 (May 1965).

8. Hoover, Edgar M. *The Location of Economic Activity*. New York: McGraw-Hill, 1948.

    This is the first book to read on location theory. The role of transportation in regional economics is discussed in both a static and a dynamic context. See especially Chapter 10.

9. ____. *Location Theory and the Shoe and Leather Industries*. Cambridge: Harvard University Press, 1937.

    This book combines the Weberian theory of firms with the market area analysis. Economics of concentration are analyzed and three concepts developed: Large-scale economies, localization economies and urbanization economies.

10. Isard, Walter. *Location and Space Economy*. New York: Wiley and the Technology Press of M. I. T., 1956.

    Various approaches to location and localization theories are considered.

In particular see Chapter 3 which discusses the rank-size rule and gravity models.

11. _____. *Methods of Regional Analysis: An Introduction to Regional Science.* New York: Wiley and the Technology Press of M. I. T., 1960.

This book is a compilation of the various techniques of regional analysis, and the most complete textbook in the field. A good bibliography is included.

12. Isard, Walter, and M. J. Peck. "Location Theory and International and Interregional Trade Theory." *Quarterly Journal of Economics*, Vol. 68, No. 1 (Feb., 1954).

This article criticizes traditional trade theory for lack of distance consideration and integrates trade and location theory through the introduction of transportation costs and the concept of opportunity cost.

13. Lathrop, George T., and John R. Hamburg, "An Opportunity-Accessibility Model for Allocating Regional Growth," *Journal of the American Institute of Planners*, Vol. 31 (May 1965).

14. Lefeber, Louis. "Regional Allocation of Resources in India." In Paul Rosenstein-Rodan, ed. *Pricing and Fiscal Policy: A Study in Method*. Cambridge: The M. I. T. Press, 1964 (also in Friedman and Alonso, ed. *Regional Development*).

The author argues that development of depressed areas may depend on the growth of industrially more advanced regions. See also by the same author, *Allocations in Space* (I. *H.* 8).

15. Lösch, August. *The Economics of Location*. (Wolfgang F. Stolper, trans.) New Haven: Yale University Press, 1954.

This book justifies central place theory through economic analysis, and is a landmark in the analysis of geographic systems of economic activities.

16. Lichtenberg, Robert M. *One Tenth of a Nation*. Cambridge: Harvard University Press, 1960.

This book analyses economic trends in the New York metropolitan region. Appendix B groups manufacturing industries by dominant locational characteristics, such as transportation and labor costs.

17. Mera, Koichi, "Efficiency and Equity in Interregional Economic Development." Doctoral dissertation, Harvard University, 1965.

This thesis is a theoretical exploration of the trade-off between national
efficiency and interregional equity. The study suggests that the loss of
efficiency in favor of interregional welfare equilization is likely to be
insignificantly small.

18. Meyer, John R. "Regional Economics: A Survey." *American Economic
Review*, Vol. LIII, No. 1 (March, 1963).

This article is an excellent non-technical discussion of the problems and
methods of regional analysis, and is very useful as a brief introduction to,
and an over-view of, the field. A good bibliography is included.

19. Mighall, Ronald L. and John D. Black. *Interregional Competition in Agriculture with Special Reference to Dairy Farming in the United States and
New England*. Cambridge: Harvard University Press, 1951.

The data used are outdated, but methodology remains appropriate.

20. Perle, Eugene D. *The Demand for Transportation: Regional and Commodity
Studies in the United States*. Chicago: University of Chicago, Department of
Geography, 1964.

21. Perloff, Harvey S. *How a Region Grows*. Committee for Economic Development Supplementary Paper No. 17. New York: The Committee, 1963.

This book is a condensation of *Regions, Resources and Economic Growth*
by Perloff, Dunn, Lampard and Muth. The data are updated and text is
less technical than the original.

22. Perloff, Harvey S. and Lowdon Wingo, Jr. "Natural Resources Endowment
and Regional Economic Growth." In Joseph J. Spengler, ed. *Natural
Resources and Economic Growth*. Washington: Resources for the Future,
1961. (Also in Friedman and Alonso, eds. *Regional Development*, supra).

The authors argue that "resources endowment" continuously changes as
technology and national demand change, and that the relative advatanges
of a region depend both upon resources and access to markets.

23. Stanford Research Institute. *Review of Techniques of Regional Analysis
with Particular Emphasis on Application of these Techniques to Regional
Problems*. Menlo Park, California: Stanford Research Institute, 1962.

The title explains the contents. A good bibliography is included. The
exposition is somewhat technical, but the work is very comprehensive.

24. Ullman, Edward, "A Theory of Location for Cities." *American Journal of
Sociology*, Vol. 46, No. 6 (May, 1941). (Also in Harold M. Mayer and

Clyde F. Kohn, eds. *Readings in Urban Geography*. Chicago: University of Chicago Press, 1959).

This article is a critique of the major theories of the location of cities from von Thünen to Christaller.

25. Vernon, Raymond. *Metropolis 1985*. Cambridge: Harvard University Press, 1960.

    This book is a summary of the findings of the New York Metropolitan Region Study. The chapter on external economies is basic for an understanding of agglomeration economics.

26. Weber, Alfred. *Theory of the Location of Industries*. Chicago University Press, 1929.

    This is a pioneering work in regional economics.

27. Wein, Harold H. "Transportation and Regional Change." In National Academy of Science-National Research Council publication 841, *Transportation Design Considerations*. Washington: The Academy-Council, 1961.

    The author argues that even given the highly developed transport system in the United States, transportation may still possess significant locational leverage.

D. *Development Economics*

1. Higgins, Benjamin H. *Economic Development Principles, Problems and Policies*. New York: Norton, 1959.

*2. Hirschman, Albert O. *The Strategy of Economic Development*. New Haven: Yale University Press, 1958.

    This book is useful as an introduction to the theory of unbalanced growth. Contrary to traditional views the author asserts that a chain of disequilibria is essential for the successful development of underdeveloped nations.

3. Marglin, Stephen A., *Public Investment Criteria*, Cambridge: M.I.T. Press, 1967.

E. *Transportation, Engineering and Planning*

1. Black, Alan, "Comparison of Three Parameters of Nonresidential Trip Generation." In *Origin and Destination: Methods and Evaluation*, Highway Research Record 114, Washington: Highway Research Board, 1966.

2. Charles River Associates Incorporated. *Review of the Market for the Super-sonic Transport – Methodology and Sensitivity Analysis*. Report No. 133-1, April 1969.

    This report evaluates the demand for SST aircraft derived under various assumptions.

3. Creighton, Roger L., Krving Hoch and Morton Schneider. "The Optimum Spacing of Arterials and Expressways." *Traffic Quarterly*, Vol. 3 No. 4 (Oct. 1959).

    The minimum cost solution for a given demand is presented as the determinant of the optimum hierarchy of an urban highway system.

4. Dewey, Ralph L. "Criterion for the Establishment of an Optimum Transportation System." *American Economic Review*, Vol. 42, No. 2 (May, 1952).

    The author advocates short-run marginal cost pricing in order to achieve maximum efficiency.

5. Friedlaender, Ann F. *The Interstate Highway System*. Amsterdam: North-Holland, 1965.

    This book is a very detailed, thorough and technical evaluation of the Interstate System. The author concludes that many rural portions were economically unsound.

6. Heanue, Kevin E. and Clyde E. Pyers. "A Comparative Evaluation of Trip Distribution Procedures." In Highway Research Record No. 114, *Origin and Destination: Methods and Evaluation – 10 Reports*. Washington: Highway Research Board, 1966.

    This article presents the results of a study of the relative accuracy of the Fratar, gravity, intervening opportunities and competing opportunities trip distribution procedures. Each model was calibrated on data from the 1948 Washington O and D Study, and used to make projections to 1955.

7. Kuhn, Tillo E. *Public Enterprise Economics and Transportation Problems*. Berkeley: University of California Press, 1962.

    This book develops the application of economic principles of public decision making to transportation problems.

8. Locklin, D. Philip. *Economics of Transportation*. 6th ed. Homewood, Illinois: Richard D. Irwin, 1966.

This book is a comprehensive introduction to the economics of transportation and the history and current practices of the industry and its regulators.

9. Martin, Brian V., F. W. Memmott and A. J. Bone. *Principles and Techniques of Predicting Future Demand for Urban Area Transportation*. Cambridge: M.I.T. Department of Civil and Sanitary Engineering, Research Report No. 38, 1961.

This report is a survey and evaluation of current urban traffic prediction techniques. Traffic is regarded as a function of basic variables such as population, land use, and vehicle ownership rates, but not vice versa.

10. Martin, Brian V. and Paul O. Roberts. "The Development of a Model for the Transport Sector." Harvard Transportation and Economic Development Seminar — Discussion Paper 18. Cambridge: Harvard Transport Research Program, 1965.

11. Meyer, John R., Merton J. Peck, John Stenason and Charles Zwick. *The Economics of Competition in the Transportation Industries*. Cambridge: Harvard University Press, 1959.

This book contains supply and demand characteristics of various modes and presents policy recommendations: increased competition and less regulatory control. Although the book is concerned with national efficiency, concepts are relevant to regional development.

12. Meyer, John R., John Kain, and Martin Wohl. *The Urban Transportation Problem*. Cambridge: Harvard University Press, 1965.

This book is based on a series of factual analyses of the problems of urban transportation including location trends, modal characteristics, role of technology, and policy problems.

13. Mohring, Herbert D. and Mitchell Harwitz. *Highway Benefits: An Analytical Framework*. Evanston: Northwestern University Press for The Transportation Center at Northwestern University, 1962.

See in particular Chapter III which presents a programming model for making transport investment decisions and Chapter I which discusses highway benefits.

14. Nelson, James C. *Railroad Transportation and Public Policy*. Washington: Brookings Institution, 1959.

This book presents a full-scale discussion of the problems of the railroad industry. Less regulation and appropriate user charges are proposed.

15. Oi, Walter Y., and Paul W. Shuldiner, *An Analysis of Urban Travel Demands*, Evanston: Northwestern University Press, 1962.

16. Polenske, Karen R. "The Study of Transportation Requirements Using National and Multiregional Input-Output Techniques." Prepared for U.S. Department of Transportation, Springfield, Va.: Clearinghouse for Federal, Scientific and Technical Information, Report No. PB 174742 (April 1967).

17. Roberts, Paul O., P. N. Taborga and Robert E. Burns. "A Model for the Formulation of Transport Alternatives." Paper presented to the American Society of Civil Engineers Conference, Miami, Florida, January 1966.

18. Ruiter, Earl R., "Improvements in Understanding, Calibrating, and Applying the Opportunity Model." In *Origin and Destination Advances in Transportation Planning*, Highway Research Record 165. Washington: Highway Research Board, 1967.

19. Southeastern Wisconsin Regional Planning Commission, "Land Use-Transportation Study: Forecasts and Alternative Plans, 1990." In *Planning Report No. 7*, Vol. 2, Waukesha, June 1966.

20. Systems Analysis and Research Corporation. *Demand for Intercity Passenger Travel in the Washington-Boston Corridor*. Report to the U. S. Department of Commerce. Parts IV and V. Washington, 1963.

    A pioneer document on behavioral demand for transportation.

21. Tinbergen, J. "The Appraisal of Road Construction: Two Calculation Schemes." *Review of Economics and Statistics*, Vol. 39, No. 3 (August 1957).

    This article presents two methods of evaluation which take into account the indirect effects of a proposed project.

22. Troxel, Emory. *Economics of Transport*. New York: Rinehart and Co., 1955.

    This is a textbook on the subject with emphasis on the relationship between transportation and spatial distribution.

F. The Economic Base

1. Andrews, Richard B. "Mechanics of the Economic Base." Series of articles in *Land Economics*, Vol. 29 through 31, (May, 1953 to Feb., 1956).

These articles are a full scale discussion of economic base theory.

2. Blumenfeld, Hans. "The Economic Base of the Metropolis." *Journal of the American Institute of Planners*, Vol. 21, No. 4 (Fall, 1955).

   This article is a criticism of the traditional "base method." The author reverses the implications of the concept and argues that it is the service sector which determines the level of activity.

3. Leontief, Wassily and Walter Isard. "The Extension of Input and Output Techniques to Interregional Analysis." In Wassily Leontief, ed. *Studies in the Structure of the American Economy*, Part II. New York: Oxford University Press, 1953.

   This article presents the first application of input-output technique to regional analysis.

4. Metzler, L. A. "A Multiple Region Theory of Income and Trade." *Econometrica*. Vol. 18, No. 4 (Oct., 1950).

   The author extends the Keynesian multiplier to a multi-region case. Stability is shown to depend on marginal propensity-to-spend of the region.

5. Thomas, Morgan D. "The Export Base and Development Stages Theories of Regional Economic Growth: An Appraisal." *Land Economics*, Vol. 40, No. 4 (Nov. 1964).

   The development stages and export-base theories are reviewed and criticized as explanatory theories of regional growth. Improvements and a possible fusion are suggested.

6. Tiebout, Charles M. *The Community Economic Base Study*. Committee for Economic Development Supplementary Paper No. 16. New York: The Committee, 1962.

   This is a textbook of the techniques of economic base analysis written for non-economists.

*7. ____. "Exports and Regional Economic Growth." *Journal of Political Economy*, Vol. 64, No. 2 (April, 1956). (Also in Friedman and Alonso, eds. *Regional Development*, supra).

   The author argues that regional growth is determined by the ability to develop an export base, but that nature of residentiary activity is a key factor in causing growth.

G. Roles and Impacts of Transportation

a. General
1. Borchert, John R. "American Metropolitan Evolution." *Geographical Review*, July, 1967.

    This article is a historical analysis of impacts of technological changes in transportation on the geographical distribution of urban centers in the United States.

2. Chinitz, Benjamin. "City and Suburb." In Benjamin Chinitz, ed. *City and Suburb: The Economics of Metropolitan Growth*. Englewood Cliffs: Prentice-Hall, 1964.

    This article is a unique and comprehensive guide to trends in metropolitan growth.

3. _____. *Freight and the Metropolis*. Cambridge: Harvard University Press, 1960.

    A non-technical but comprehensive analysis of the role of transportation in the economy of the New York Metropolitan region is presented. This book is a prototype of how the role of transportation can be analyzed in a regional context.

4. Clark, Colin. "Transport: Maker and Breaker of Cities." *Town Planning Review*, Vol. 28, No. 4 (Jan., 1958).

    This article is a summary of effects of improved transport system on spatial distribution of activity. The author argues that except for a very few heavy industries, old ideas about transport costs are inapplicable.

5. Cooley, Charles H. "The Theory of Transportation." *Publications of the American Economic Association*, Vol. 9, No. 3 (May, 1894).

    This article is a well-known classic in the field of transportation and the location of cities. The author argues that population and wealth generally collect at breaks in the transport system.

6. Fogel, Robert W. *Railways and American Economic Growth: Essays in Econometric History*. Baltimore: Johns Hopkins Press, 1964.

    A quantitative estimate of the social savings generated by the railroads during the nineteenth century is presented. The author's viewpoint is unique, but his methodology and conclusions disputable.

*7. Hunter, Holland. "Resources, Transportation and Economic Development," in Joseph J. Spengler, ed. *National Resources and Economic Growth*, Washington: Resources for the Future, 1961.

This article examines the role of transportation on the development of underdeveloped countries.

8. Machlup, Fritz. *The Basing-point System*. Philadelphia: The Blakeston Company, 1949.

Chapter I discusses the locational effects of this pricing scheme.

9. Owen, Wilfred. "Transportation and Economic Development." *American Economic Review*, Vol. 49, No. 2 (May, 1959).

This article is a concise description of the role of transportation in underdeveloped countries. The optimal amount of transport investment, modal choice, and the demand for transport are discussed.

10. Pegrum, Dudley F. *Urban Transportation and the Location of Industry in Metropolitan Los Angeles*. Los Angeles: University of California, Bureau of Business and Economic Research, 1963.

The author concludes that industries in the area are clustered along the railroad lines laid out before 1920, although there is a noticeable tendency for dispersion from the central city.

11. Ullman, Edward L. "The Role of Transportation and the Basis for Interaction;" in William L. Thomas, Jr., ed. *Man's Role in Changing the Face of the Earth*. Chicago: University of Chicago Press, 1956.

This article, written for non- and semi-professionals, is an excellent guide to the impact of transportation on the spatial distribution of activity.

12. United States Congress. House of Representatives. *Economic and Social Effects of Highway Improvement*: Part IV of the Final Report of the Highway Cost Allocation Study. 87th Congress. 1st Session. House Document No. 54. Washington: GPO, 1961.

Various types of highway non-vehicular benefits are discussed.

13. Willson, George W., Barbara R. Bergmann, Leon V. Hirsch, and Martin S. Klein. *The Impact of Highway Investment on Development*. Washington: Brookings Institution Transport Research Program, 1966.

A series of case studies is used to derive a general theory of transport effects on underdeveloped countries. In addition to purely economic impacts, spill-over effects such as education are emphasized.

14. Zettel, Richard M. "Ten Notes on Transportation and Economic Development." Mimeographed. Berkeley: University of California, Institute of Traffic and Transportation Research, 1961.

This article is a concise and well thought out statement of the role of transportation in the economy.

b.   Impact Studies

*1. Bone, A. J. and Martin Wohl. "Massachusetts Route 128 Impact Study." In National Academy of Science, Highway Research Board Bulletin No. 227, *Highways and Economic Development.* Washington: Highway Research Board, 1959.

This article is a prototype of large-scale highway impact study, and is outstanding both for the comprehensiveness of the variables surveyed and the large area included in the study.

2.   Bureau of Socio-Economic Research, Inc. *Socio-Economic Impact of Massachusetts Route 495.* Prepared for Commonwealth of Massachusetts, Department of Public Works and U.S. Department of Commerce, Bureau of Public Roads, 1963 through 1964.

This is a series of four reports on impact of Mass. Route 495 by Bone and Wohl. See in particular, Report No. 1, *Reference Guide to Methodology,* Feb. 1963.

3.   CONSAD Research Corporation, "Design for Impact Studies," Northeast Corridor Transportation Project, Processed. Washington: CONSAD Research Corporation, 1965.

4.   Garrison, William L. and Marion E. Marts. *Geographic Impact of Highway Improvements.* Seattle: University of Washington, Highway Economic Studies, 1958.

This is a thorough study of the impacts of the reorientation of U.S. Highway 99 in western Washington, and is probably the most comprehensive study of its kind.

5.   Haefele, Edwin T. ed. *Transport and National Goals.* Washington: Brookings Institution, 1969.

This book relates transport planning with other aspects of national development policy.

6. Horral, Clell G. *Preparation and Appraisal of Transport Projects.* Washington: Brookings Institution, 1965.

7. Horral, Clell G. and Tillo E. Kuhn. *Transport Planning in Developing Countries.* Washington: Brookings Institution, 1965.

8. National Academy of Science National Research Council. *Some Evaluations of Highway Improvement Impacts.* Highway Research Board Bulletin No. 268. Washington: Highway Research Board, 1960.

   This publication includes eight reports on particular highway impact studies or general evaluations of the methodology currently used in impact studies. See in particular A. S. Lang and M. Wohl "Evaluation of Highway Impact" and W. N. Nash and J. R. Voss "Analyzing the Socio-Economic Impacts of Urban Highways."

9. Putman, Stephen H. "Modeling and Evaluating the Indirect Impacts of Alternative Northeast Corridor Transportation Systems." In *Transportation System Analysis and Calculation of Alternate Plans,* Highway Research Record 180. Washington: Highway Research Board, 1967.

10. U.S. Department of Commerce, Bureau of Public Roads. *Highways and Social and Economic Change.* Washington: GPO, 1964.

    This book is a review and summary of highway impact studies sponsored by the Department of Commerce. A very comprehensive bibliography is included.

11. U.S. Congress. Hearings before a Special Sub-committee of the Senate Committee on Commerce. *Great Lakes-St. Lawrence Seaway Transportation Study.* 88th Congress. 2nd Session. Serials 55, 56, and 62. Washington: GPO, 1964.

    The hearings constitute a study of the effects of the St. Lawrence Seaway after 6 years of operation.

H. Programming Models

1. Beckman, Martin and Thomas Marschak. "An Activity Analysis Approach to Location Theory." *Kyklos,* Vol. 8 (1955).

   This article applies activity analysis to derive an efficient spatial distribution of activity. Traditional location theories are incorporated in the model.

2. Brodersohn, Mario S. "A Multi-regional Input-Output Analysis of the Argen-

tine Economy." Doctoral dissertation, Harvard University, December, 1965.

This thesis compares the accuracy of input-output models with traditional forecasting methods for the Argentine economy.

3. Dorfman, Robert, Paul A. Samuelson and Robert M. Solow. *Linear Programming and Economic Analysis.* New York: McGraw-Hill, 1958.

This is one of the best textbooks on linear programming for economists.

4. Garrison, W. L. and D. F. Marble. "Analysis of Highway Networks: A Linear Programming Formulation." *Highway Research Board Proceedings.* Vol. 37, (1958). Washington: Highway Research Board, 1958.

The problem of shipments of commodities between urban centers over a regional or national highway network is treated. Solution of the model determines the optimum allocation of funds for improvement to the highway system.

5. Harwitz, Mitchell and Arthur P. Hurter. *Transportation and the Economy of the Appalachian Region.* Transportation Center at Northwestern University Report No. 66. Prepared for the Area Redevelopment Administration, 1966.

This report develops a linear programming model which indicates the effect of an increase in productive capacity or a decrease in transport costs.

6. Henderson, James M. *The Efficiency of the Coal Industry: An Application of Linear Programming.* Cambridge: Harvard University Press, 1958.

A linear programming model is used to describe the efficiency of the coal industry.

7. Hurter, Arthur and Leon N. Moses. "Regional Investment and Interregional Programming." *Papers and Proceedings of the Regional Science Association,* Vol. 13 (1964).

An interregional programming model which is operational and is suited to partially regulated economics is presented. The model is static and seems to be too simplified for evaluating investment projects, but it is useful for testing general policies.

8. Lefeber, Louis. *Allocation in Space.* Amsterdam: North-Holland Publishing Co., 1958.

This book develops an equilibrium and a programming model of the geographic distribution of economic activity. The models are very advanced as conceptual tools.

9. Leontief, Wassily and Alan Stout. "Multi-Regional and Input-Output Analysis." In Tibor Barna, ed. *Structural Interdependence and Economic Development.* London: Macmillan, 1963.

   The authors develop an interregional input-output model and undertake a partial empirical implementation to demonstrate what data is necessary and what data is readily available.

10. Mera, Koichi. "Evaluation of Techniques for Assignment of Interregional Commodity Flows." Harvard Transportation and Economic Development Seminar Discussion Paper No. 22.

    This paper compares the accuracy of the gravity and linear programming models in distributing interregional commodity flows for several empirical cases, and develops general criteria for comparing the accuracy of these two models.

11. Polenske, Karen R. "A Case Study of Transportation Models Used in Multiregional Analysis." Doctoral dissertation, Harvard University, May, 1966.

    This thesis compares the accuracy of several interregional commodity-flow estimation models which can be used in a general equilibrium framework.

*12. Samuelson, Paul A. "Spatial Price Equilibrium and Linear Programming." *American Economic Review,* Vol. 42, No. 3 (June, 1952).

    This article demonstrates the use of linear programming in solving international or interregional trade problems.

13. Stevens, Benjamin H. "Linear Programming and Location Rent." *Journal of Regional Science,* Vol. 3, No. 2 (Winter, 1961).

    The classical theory of location is linked to the solution of the Hitchcock-Koopmans transportation problem.

I. Simulation Models

1. Bos, H. C. and L. M. Koyck. "The Appraisal of Investments in Transportation Projects: A Practical Example." Rotterdam: Netherlands Economic Institute, 1958. (Presented at the 20th European Meeting of the Economic

Society, Bilboa, September, 1958). For a brief discussion of this article, see *Econometrica,* Vol. 27, No. 4 (October, 1959) pp. 705–706.

The authors use four models to find the total effect on an underdeveloped country of undertaking a single transportation project. The models give widely different results.

2. Bouchard, Richard J. and Clyde E. Pyers. "Use of Gravity Model for Describing Urban Travel." In Highway Research Record No. 88, *Travel Patterns – 8 Reports.* Publication No. 1304. Washington: The Academy Council, 1964.

This article evaluates the gravity model as an analytical tool for stimulating present and forecasting future urban trip distribution patterns.

3. Harris, Britton. "Experiments in Projection of Transportation and Land Use." *Traffic Quarterly,* Vol. XVI, No. 2 (April 1962).

This article describes the urban land-use/transportation model used in the Penn-Jersey Study. A significant feature of this model is the interdependence between transportation and land use.

4. Charles River Associates. *A Model of Urban Passenger Travel Demand in the San Francisco Metropolitan Area.* Report 117-1. Cambridge: Charles River Associates, 1967.

This report presents a general passenger transportation demand model applicable to an urban context. Parameters are estimated for various modes and trip purposes.

5. Fratar, Thomas J. "Vehicular Trip Distribution by Successive Approximation." *Traffic Quarterly,* Vol. VIII, No. 1 (Jan. 1954).

A method is presented for assigning trips to routes when trip generation at each node is known.

6. Kain, John F. "The Development of Urban Transportation Models." *Papers and Proceedings of the Regional Science Association,* Vol. 19 (1965).

This article is a presentation of the objectives and summaries of the RAND Corporation urban transportation model.

7. Kain, John F., and John R. Meyer. "Computer Simulations, Physio-economic Systems, and Intraregional Models." American Economic Association, Papers and Proceedings of the Eightieth Annual Meeting, 1967.

8. Kresge, David. "A Simulation Model for Development Programming." Harvard Transportation and Economic Development Seminar Discussion Paper No. 32, Nov., 1965.

This paper develops an aggregate simulation model which includes a detailed sectoral analysis.

*9. Mathematica ed. *Studies in Travel Demand.* 3 Volumes. Princeton: Mathematica, 1966, 1967.

10. Meyer, John R., David Kresge, and Paul O. Roberts. *Techniques of Transport Planning.* Washington: The Brookings Institution, 1971. Vol. II.

11. Roberts, Paul O. "The Role of Transport in Developing Countries: A Development Planning Model." Harvard Transportation and Economic Development Seminar Discussion Paper No. 40, May, 1966.

Transport simulation model which can be used alone, or in conjunction with the macro model given, is presented.

12. Roberts, Paul O. "Transport Planning: Models for Developing Countries." Doctoral dissertation, Northwestern University, Department of Civil Engineering, June, 1966.

This thesis formulates a simulation for use in evaluating transport investments for underdeveloped countries and presents a synthesis of several transport planning models.

13. Steger, William A., "The Pittsburgh Urban Renewal Simulation Model," *Journal of the American Institute of Planners,* Vol. 31, (May 1965).

14. U.S. Bureau of Public Roads, *Calibrating and Testing a Gravity Model with a Small Computer,* Washington: Government Printing Office, July 1963.

15. Voorhees, Alan M., ed. *Land Use and Traffic Models.* Journal of the American Institute of Planners, Vol. 28, No. 2 (May, 1959, Special Issue).

This issue is a collection of articles on land use and traffic projections.

II. Metropolitan Transportation

1. Berry, Donald S, G. W. Blomme, P. W. Shuldiner, and J. H. Jones. *The Technology of Urban Transportation.* Evanston: Northwestern University

Press for the Transportation Center at Northwestern University, 1963.

This book is essentially a catalogue of costs and performance characteristics of currently available urban transportation modes.

2. Committee for Economic Development. *Developing Metropolitan Transportation Policies: A Guide for Local Leadership.* New York: The Committee, 1965.

    This book presents a good overview of the problems in urban transportation. Policy statement emphasizes process of decision-making, financing methods and intergovernmental relationships.

3. Domencich, Thomas A., Gerald Kraft, and Jean-Paul Valette, "Estimation of Urban Passenger Travel Behavior: An Economic Demand Model." In *Transportation System Evaluation,* Highway Research Record 238. Washington: Highway Research Board, 1968.

4. Fitch, Lyle C., and Associates. *Urban Transportation and Public Policy.* San Francisco: Chandler Publishing Co., 1964.

5. Garrison, William L. "Intra- and Interurban Transportation Networks." In Forrest R. Pitts, ed. *Urban Systems and Economic Development.* Eugene, Ore.: University of Oregon, School of Business Administration, 1962.

    The effect of transport networks on the spacing of urban centers and policy criteria for choosing a transport system are discussed.

6. Irwin, N. A. "Review of Existing Land-Use Forecasting Techniques." In Highway Research Record No. 88. *Travel Patterns: 8 Reports.* Washington: The Academy-Council, 1965.

    The review covers fourteen techniques which range from the operational to the conceptual. Many of these are found to be insensitive to changes in accessibility.

7. Kraft, Gerald. "Economic Aspects of Urban Passenger Transportation." In *Transportation Economics,* Highway Research Record 285, Washington: Highway Research Board, 1969.

8. Kraft, Gerald, and Martin Wohl. "Special Survey Paper: New Directions for Passenger Demand Analysis and Forecasting." *Transportation Research,* Vol. 1, November, 1967.

    A good discussion of how behavioral models should be developed and applied to urban passenger demand forecasting.

9. Kuhn, Tillo E. "The Economics of Transportation Planning in Urban Areas." In *Transportation Economics*. New York: Columbia University Press for the National Bureau of Economic Research, 1965.

10. Liepman, Kate K. *The Journey to Work*. New York: Oxford University Press, 1944.

This book is a non-technical discussion of the behavioral variables influencing mode choice for the journey to work.

11. Meyer, John R., John F. Kain and Martin Wohl. *The Urban Transportation Problem*. Cambridge: Harvard University Press, 1965.

This is the basic reference on urban transportation.

12. National Committee on Urban Transportation. *Better Transportation for Your City: A Guide to the Factual Development of Urban Transportation Plans*. Chicago: Public Administration Service, 1958.

This book is a guide to planning urban transportation written for non-professionals.

13. Oi, Walter T. and Paul W. Shuldiner. *An Analysis of Urban Travel Demands*. Evanston: Northwestern University Press for the Transportation Center at Northwestern University, 1962.

This book is a statistical analysis of urban traffic generation. Household size, car ownership, distance from the C.B.D. and residential density are examined as explanatory variables.

14. Penn-Jersey Transportation Study, Vol. I, II, and III. Sponsored by Commonwealth of Pennsylvania and State of New Jersey in cooperation with the U.S. Department of Commerce, Bureau of Public Roads, 1964.

This is a good example of a recent large-scale transportation study. The reports are nontechnical, and generally present only the results of the study, rather than its methods.

15. Shuldiner, Paul W. "Land Use, Activity and Non-Residential Trip Generation." In *Origin and Destination: Methods and Evaluation. Highway Research Record* 114. Washington: Highway Research Board, 1966.

16. Strotz, Robert H., "Urban Transportation Parables." In Julius Margolis, ed., *The Public Economy of Urban Communities*. Baltimore: Johns Hopkins Press for Resources for the Future, 1965.

17. Taaffe, Edward J., Barry J. Garner and Maurice H. Yeates. *The Peripheral Journey to Work: A Geographic Consideration.* Evanston: Northwestern University Press for the Transportation Center at Northwestern University, 1963.

This book is a study in geographical variations in commuting patterns.

18. Thompson, William R. *A Preface to Urban Economics: Towards a Conceptual Framework for Study and Research.* Washington: Resources for the Future, 1963.

A comprehensive approach to the topic of urban economics is developed.

19. U.S. National Capital Transportation Agency. *Appendix to Nov. 1, 1962, Report to the President − Vol. IV: A Model for Estimating Travel Model Usage.*

A model based on empirically estimated "diversion curves" and some results are presented.

20. Voorhees, Alan M. "A General Theory of Traffic Movement." Institute of Traffic Engineers. Proceedings, 1955. New Haven, Connecticut.

This article is a classic in the analysis of urban transportation. The frequency distribution of various types of trips, the pulls of competing destinations, and the mode of travel are considered.

21. Voorhees, Alan M. and Associates. Travel Forecast Study, Commonwealth of Massachusetts, Eastern Massachusetts Regional Planning Project: Progress Report for December, 1965.

This report contained a multiple regression traffic projection model.

22. Warner, Stanley L. *Stochastic Choice of Mode in Urban Travel: A Study in Binary Choice.* Evanston: Northwestern University, 1962.

This book is a statistical examination of consumers' modal choice for urban transportation using time, cost and income as independent variables.

23. Zettel, Richard M., and Richard R. Carll. *Summary Review of Major Metropolitan Area Transportation Studies in the United States.* Institute of Transportation and Traffic Engineering, Special Report. Berkeley: University of California, November, 1962.

See also: I. *E.* 1, 6, 9 and 18   I. *G.* b 1 and 2
          I. *G.* a 1, 2, 3, 4 and 10   I. *I.* 2, 4, 5 and 6

III. Rates, Regulations, and Pricing Policies

1. Caves, Richard E. *Air Transportation and its Regulators.* Cambridge: Harvard University Press, 1962.

   This book is the most comprehensive guide available on the regulation of air transport.

2. Daggett, Stuart. *Principles of Inland Transportation.* 4th ed. New York: Harper & Brothers, 1955.

   See Chapters 18 and 19 for a thorough discussion of the varieties of competition in transportation, group, and basing point rates and long-haul, short-haul price discrimination.

3. Dean, Joel. "Cost Analysis for Competitive Railroad Rate-Making." In Karl M. Ruppenthal, ed. *Issues in Transportation Economics.* Columbus, Ohio: Charles E. Merrill, 1965.

   This article gives the reasons, including rate policy, for rail's loss of traffic.

4. Garfield, Paul J., and Wallace F. Lovejoy. *Public Utility Economics."* Englewood Cliffs: Prentice-Hall, 1964.

   This book is oriented to the public utilities, particularly gas, but Chapters 10 and 11 present a good discussion of various pricing policies.

5. Levine, Michael E. "Is Regulation Necessary? California Air Transportation and National Regulatory Policy." *Yale Law Journal,* Vol. 74, No. 8 (July, 1965).

   The experience of air travel on the Los Angeles-San Francisco route is used to argue for less control of the airline industry.

6. Lindahl, Martin L. "The Anti-Trust Laws and Transportation." *The Anti-Trust Bulletin,* Vol. XI, Nos. 1 and 2 (Jan.-Apr., 1966).

   This article is a survey of the applicability of anti-trust laws to the transport industry. The author points out that a very strict application of anti-trust laws to promote competition is not always warranted.

7. Machlup, Fritz. *The Basing Point System.* Philadelphia: The Blakeston Company, 1949.

   This book is an analysis of the basing point system of rate making and its consequences.

8. Meyer, John R., David Kresge, and Paul O. Roberts. *Techniques of Transport Planning.* Washington: The Brookings Institution, 1971. Vol. I.

9. Nelson, James C. "The Princing of Highway, Waterway and Airway Facilities." American Economic Association — Papers and Proceedings of the 74th Annual Meeting, 1961.

10. Nelson, James R. "Pricing Transport Services" in Gary Fromm, ed. *Transport Investment and Economic Development.* Washington: Brookings Institution, 1965.

11. Peck, Merton J. "Competitive Policy for Transportation;" in Almarin Phillips, ed. *Perspectives on Anti-Trust Policy.* Princeton: Princeton University Press, 1965.

    The author considers the extent to which competition can be substituted for regulation in transportation.

12. Pegrum, Dudley F. *Transportation: Economics and Public Policy.* Homewood, Illinois: Richard D. Irwin, 1963.

    This is a basic textbook on rates and regulations.

13. Roberts, Merrill, J. "Transport Costs, Pricing and Regulation." In Universities-National Bureau Committee for Economic Research, *Transportation Economics.* New York: National Bureau of Economic Research, 1965.

    This article is a rather technical discussion of the relationship of costs to rates in the railroad industry.

14. Rose, Joseph R. "Regulation of Rates and Intermodal Transport Competition." I.C.C. *Practitioners Journal,* Vol. 33, No. 1 (October, 1965).

    This article presents a brief discussion of rate policies to promote intermodal competition.

15. Sampson, Roy J. and Martin T. Farris. *Domestic Transportation: Practice, Theory and Policy.* Boston: Houghton Mifflin Co., 1966.

    Chapters 9–12 give an excellent and fairly nontechnical presentation of essential background on rate making.

16. Transportation Center at Northwestern University. *Private and Unregulated Carriers: A Conference.* Evanston: Northwestern University Press, 1963.

This is a series of articles on various aspects of unregulated carriers. See in particular G. W. Hilton "Transportation Regulation and Private Carriage" and R. A. Nelson "The Concept of the Common Carrier Today."

17. Vickrey, William, "Pricing as a Tool in Coordination of Local Transportation." In *Transportation Economics.* New York: Columbia University Press for the National Bureau of Economic Research, 1965.

18. Williams, Ernest W., Jr. and David W. Bluestone. *Rationale of Federal Transportation Policy.* Washington: U.S. Department of Commerce, April, 1960.

This book gives a brief survey of current Commerce Department views on a number of problems in rate making, entry control, and subsidies.

19. ——. *The Regulation of Rail-Motor Rate Competition.* New York: Harper and Brothers, 1958.

This book is a detailed critique of the I.C.C.'s rate making and entry control policies with respect to rail and motor carriers.

20. United States Interstate Commerce Commission, Bureau of Transport Economics and Statistics. "Value of Service in Rate Making." Statement No. 5912 (mimeo). Washington: The Commission, 1959.

An elaborate description of value-of-service as an element in I.C.C.'s rate making principles is presented.

21. Wilson, George. "The Effect of Rate Regulation on Resource Allocation in Transportation." *American Economic Review,* Vol. LIV, No. 3 (May, 1964).

This article analyzes several different rate principles used by the I.C.C. and examines their implications for the division of traffic between rail, motor and water carriers.

IV. Technology and Costs

1. Allman, Leslie C. "Containerization and Logistics." In Karl M. Ruppenthal, ed. *Transportation Frontiers.* Stanford: Stanford University Graduate School of Business, 1962.

This article presents a useful although somewhat general description of present and future container possibilities.

2. Buford, Curtis D. "New Concepts in Railroading." In Karl M. Ruppenthal, ed. *Transportation Frontiers.* Stanford: Stanford Graduate School of Business, 1962.

    A good catalogue of railroad innovations to 1962 is presented. The author argues that regulatory constraints may retard innovation and development.

3. Charles River Associates Incorporated. "Choice of Transport Technology under Varying Factor Endowments in Less Developed Countries." Unpublished report prepared for the Office of Assistant Secretary for Policy and International Affairs — Department of Transportation. Washington, 1969.

    This report develops a framework for the economic evaluation of alternative transport projects. It incorporates the conceptual methodology in a set of computer programs.

4. Howard, Lee, R. and James I. Williams. " 'SST' Prospectus — Economics of the United States 'SST'." *Lockheed Horizons,* Autumn, 1965.

    This article gives a cogent discussion of manufacturer's forecast of the SST's impact and of the market for the aircraft.

5. Massachusetts Institute of Technology Interdepartmental Systems Design Course Student Project. *The Glideway System: A Highspeed Ground Transportation System for the Northeast Corridor of the United States.* Cambridge: M.I.T., 1965.

    This report is an engineering-economic analysis of a high speed passenger system for the Boston-Washington corridor and is an excellent example of systems approach to planning, although conclusions are disputable.

6. Meyer, John R., and Gerald Kraft. "The Evaluation of Statistical Costing Techniques as Applied in the Transportation Industry." American Economic Association — Papers and Proceedings of the 73rd Annual Meeting, 1960. (*American Economic Review.* Vol. 51. May, 1961).

7. National Academy of Sciences–National Research Council. *Science and Technology in the Railroad Industry:* A Report to the Secretary of Commerce by the Committee on Science and Technology in the Railroad Industry of the National Academy of Sciences–National Research Council Washington: The Academy–Council, 1963.

    This report is an evaluation of R & D in the U.S. railroads as of 1963.

8. ——. *Inland and Maritime Transportation of Unitized Cargo:* Academy–Council, 1963.

Summaries of the costs of break-bulk, palletized, and containerized cargo movement as applied to maritime general cargo are presented. Appendices E, F, and G are useful for definitions.

9. ———. Maritime Cargo Transportation Conference. *Recent Research in Maritime Transportation.* Publication 592, Washington: The Academy-Council, 1958.

This book contains a series of articles on various aspects of containerization and other maritime research.

10. Nelson, Robert S., and Edward M. Johnson, eds. *Technological Change and the Future of the Railways.* Selected papers from a three-day conference conducted by the Transportation Center at Northwestern University. Evanston: The Center, 1961.

This book is a good survey of technological trends in the railroads as of 1961.

11. Owen, Wilfred. *Strategy for Mobility.* Washington: The Brookings Institution Transport Research Program, 1964.

See Chapter IV, "Choice of Technology," for the relevance of technological trends to development.

12. Railway Systems and Management Association. *The Developing Transportation Revolution.* Chicago: The Association, 1960.

This book contains a series of articles on railroad handling techniques. In particular, see Macomber, "An Overall View of Unit Loading."

13. ———. *Integral Trains.* Chicago: The Association, 1963.

This book contains a series of articles on integral trains taken from talks by management. In particular see, Cripe, and F. S. Macomber.

14. ———. *Railway Equipment Strategy.* Chicago: The Association, 1962.

This book contains a series of articles on railroad innovation. See Hamilton on the importance of R & D to the railroad industry.

15. Ruppenthal, Karl M., ed. *Transportation Frontiers.* Stanford: Stanford University Graduate School of Business, 1962.

This book, a collection of papers from a National Defense Transportation Association meeting at Stanford University, April, 1962, discusses in general terms advances in technology and their applications, and is useful for background information.

16. Sharp, Clifford. *The Problem of Transport.* London: Pergamon Press, 1965.

This book is good background for general analysis.

17. Shoup, Donald. "Port Operations and Economic Development." Doctoral dissertation, Harvard University, 1966.

This thesis discusses the implications of containers and surface effect vehicles.

18. Soberman, Richard M. "A Railway Performance Model." Harvard Transportation and Economic Development Seminar — Discussion Paper 45. Cambridge: Harvard Transport Research Program, August, 1965.

19. ——. *Transport Technology for Developing Regions: A Study of Road Transportation in Venezuela.* Cambridge: M.I.T. Press, 1966.

20. Straszheim, Mahlon R. *The International Airline Industry.* Washington: The Brookings Institution, 1969.

This book describes the structure of the airline industry and suggests policies which would improve efficiency in the industry.

21. Zane, Edward Allen. *Trailer-on-Flatcar: An Economic Analysis of Piggyback Transport in New England.* Boston: Federal Reserve Bank of Boston, 1964.

An excellent treatment of cost history and some implications of piggyback are presented.

Availability of Transport Statistics

The most useful transportation statistics for work in regional development are those giving the origins and destinations of passenger and freight movements.

Fairly comprehensive (but far from complete) origin and destination data for passengers are available only for *commercial* airline transportation. After over a century of selling tickets on an origin-destination basis, such data are still not available for railroad passenger travel. Passenger automobile travel, which accounts for about 90 percent of all passenger-miles, both within metropolitan regions and intercity, has been sampled on a flow basis at many times and in many places. The results are generally useful only in terms of link density, but reasonably good origin and destination data do exist for several cities.[1]

Some origin-destination data are available for rail freight movements. The Carload Waybill Sample (V.B.3), published by the Interstate Commerce Commission, gives this information for rail common carriers. This sample is broken down in a variety of ways. The most generally useful for regional development is the series of state-to-state movements of rail freight, which has been published annually since World War II. This series appears in two forms: in an abbreviated form, giving all origins and destinations by state and by major commodity groups; and in a six-volume form, which has a much more detailed commodity breakdown. These volumes give, by destination and commodity subclassification, the following information: state of origin, number of carloads recorded in the sample, average weight of shipment per carload, average distance traveled per ton and per car, and receipts per car, per ton, per car-mile and per ton-mile. The Carload Waybill Sample also includes separate volumes which give generally the same information for shipments moving within and between ratemaking regions. Finally, the sample is broken down into a series by distance of shipment. This series makes it possible to compare the characteristics of rail shipment distances for any region, or a sample from direct observation, with the national average with respect to variables such as average revenue per ton-mile and average revenue tons per car for specified distances.

Considerable information on types of freight shipped, tonnages handled, and revenues may also be found in the reports of individual carriers to the ICC. The Commission summarizes this material in two annual series: one for all forms of transportation (II.4 all parts) and another for railroad freight transportation statistics (V.B.4).

Additional information on costs can be obtained from the ICC's annual reports for particular commodities, loading, and types of shipments. These data are available for both rail and truck and are issued for both the country as a whole and for large regions. The railroad cost data are taken from Form A and must be used with a degree of caution. Although the ICC has tried to separate marginal costs from average costs, the effort has not been completely successful.

Data for freight moving by truck are also available on an area basis. But these are not nearly as useful or reliable as the rail data, for the following reasons: (1) The Interstate Commerce Commission has no jurisdiction over, and collects no data from, private truckers or common carriers operating entirely within one state. Although no one knows the exact tonnages moving by private truck, it is probable that private truck ton-miles are of the same order of magnitude as

---

1. See, for example, Wilbur Smith and Associates, *Comprehensive Traffic and Transportation Inventory: Final Report to the Commonwealth of Massachusetts, Boston Regional Planning Project.*

common-carrier ton-miles. Therefore the lack of detailed information is serious. (2) The Interstate Commerce Commission publishes no detailed information on the activities of contract-carrier trucks. These are much less important than either common or private carriers in terms of total ton-miles hauled, but they are very important for some major types of truck shipment (e.g., petroleum products and automobiles). (3) Even for common carriers, truck information is available only on the basis of the area in which the headquarters of the truck line is located. Since truck hauls are typically shorter than rail hauls, even freight information classified on the basis of the location of the truck headquarters may tell much of the geographical story. But it is probably least likely to do so for relatively remote areas, including areas which raise special problems of economic development precisely because they are remote.

In conclusion, the following may be said about transportation statistics:

1. Either on a general or an origin-and-destination basis, passenger statistics are less complete and useful than freight statistics. The principal reason for this difference is the overwhelming dominance of the private automobile in passenger transportation. Private trucking is important in the movement of goods. but it is far less important. The exception to this generality is found in aviation. Commercial aviation passenger data are available, in great detail, on an origin-and-destination as ticketed basis. But, even here, detailed data account for only a fraction of total movements by plane. Most flights (but not most passenger miles) are accounted for by general aviation.

2. Railroad freight statistics are more useful than those available for any other mode. The only possible exception involves domestic waterborne commerce, for which very detailed statistics of cargoes landed and loaded are available port-by-port. For some commodities with limited origins or destinations, these statistics can be made to yield origin-and-destination data. But, in general, this is not possible. Common carrier statistics are much more complete, for all modes of transport, than other statistics; and railroad freight movements are dominated to a unique degree by common carriers. In addition, the Interstate Commerce Commission's various compilations of Carload Waybill Statistics for railroads have no counterparts in other modes of transport.

I. Air Transportation

1. U.S. Civil Aeronautics Board. *Competition Among Domestic Air Carriers.* Quarterly with annual summary beginning 1960.

Gives origins and destinations by cities of U.S. air passenger traffic. Based on title below.

2. U.S. Civil Aeronautics Board. *Handbook of Airline Statistics.* Annual.

   Extensive data on costs, revenue, and total volume by carrier. Passengers and freight separated, but no commodity break-down. Includes figures from 1926 for certified carriers, and past ten years for non-certified.

3. U.S. Civil Aeronautics Board and U.S. Federal Aviation Agency. *Domestic Origin and Destination Survey of Airline Passenger Traffic.* Quarterly.

   Origins and destinations of U.S. air passenger traffic compiled from a 10 percent sample. The series includes an international origin and destination survey.

4. U.S. Federal Aviation Administration. *Airport Activity Statistics of Certified Route Air Carriers.* Semiannual.

   Gives cargo ton-miles by city of origin. No commodity breakdown or destinations given.

II. Motor Transport

1. American Trucking Association. *American Trucking Trends.* Annual.

   Oriented to financial aspect, but contains data on length of haul and a commodity breakdown of intercity cargo hauled by certified truck carriers.

2. ———. *Intercity Truck Tonnage.* Quarterly, with annual summary.

   Gives tonnage hauled by type of certified carrier for 9 U.S. regions.

3. U.S. Bureau of Public Roads (Now, Federal Highway Administration). *Highway Statistics.* Annual.

   Primarily oriented to revenues and taxes, but gives a regional breakdown of average loads, vehicle miles, and frequency of heavy loads on main rural roads.

4. U.S. Interstate Commerce Commisson, Bureau of Accounts. *Annual Transport Statistics in the United States, Part 7: Motor Carriers.*

   Gives revenues and costs of trucking by regions.

For a discussion of trucking data collected in the 1963 Census of Transportation see Donald E. Church, "New Trucking Data from 1963 Census of Transportation," in Highway Research Record No. 82, *Freight Transportation – 9 Reports,* Publication 1267, (Washington: National Academy of Sciences–National Research Council, 1965). For an article on the problems in using highway ton-mile statistics, see in the same publication, Alexander French, "Highway Ton-Miles."

III. Metropolitan Transportation

1. American Transit Association. *Transit Fact Book.* Annual.

    Gives total figures for several years on passengers, revenue, some cost items, and track and route mileage.

2. U.S. Bureau of the Census. *U.S. Census of Population: 1960. Final Report PC(2)-6B Subject Reports. Journey to Work.*

    Most comprehensive source on use of urban transit systems. Gives modal split by income, occupation, and area of residency for all SMSAs.

IV. Pipelines

1. U.S. Interstate Commerce Commission, Bureau of Accounts. *Transport Statistics in the United States, Part 6: Oil Pipelines.*

    Data by carrier on total volume, revenues and costs.

    For information on the gas industry in general see American Gas Association, *Gas Facts* (Annual), and for similar data on the petroleum industry see American Petroleum Institute, *Petroleum Facts and Figures.*

V. Railroads

A. Use of Waybill Statistics

1. Association of Interstate Commerce Commission Practitioners. *Report on Waybill Statistics and their Utilization.* Washington: The Association, 1954.

    Should be read in conjunction with ICC report on the same topic.

2. Clark, Jere W. "Rail Freight Data: A Tool for Market and Regional Analysis."

Southern Economic Journal, Vol. XXIII, No. 2 (October, 1956).

Describes possible research uses of ICC's *Carload Waybill Statistics.*

3. Rosander, A. C. "Obtaining Acceptable Quality Data from Carload Waybill and Other Samples." In Highway Research Record No. 82, *Freight Transportation – 9 Reports.* Publication 1267. Washington: National Academy of Sciences–National Research Council, 1965.

This article describes the factors that determine the quality of data obtained from a probability sample, with special reference to the ICC carload waybill sample.

4. U.S. Interstate Commerce Commission. Bureau of Transport Economics and Statistics. "Waybill Statistics: Their History and Use." Statement No. 543 (mimeo). Washington: The Commission, 1954.

Title explains.

B. Railway Statistics

1. Association of American Railroads. Bureau of Railway Economics. *Statistics of Railroads of Class I in the United States.* Annual.

Includes data for preceding ten years. Gives a very detailed breakdown of total volume by commodities and some cost and revenue data.

2. U.S. Interstate Commerce Commission, Bureau of Accounts, *Transport Statistics in the United States. Part I: Railroads.*

Statistics on costs by region. Oriented heavily to financial aspects, but gives some data on scope of the railroad system by regions

3. ——, Bureau of Economics, *Carload Waybill Statistics* for years 1947–1966.

Department of Transportation, Office of Secretary, *Carload Waybill Statistics,* 1969.

——, Federal Railroad Administration, *Carload Waybill Statistics,* 1970 ff.

Very detailed and comprehensive survey of freight origins and destinations.

In 1966 this series was discontinued by the ICC. The Department of Transportation issued a series in 1969 from the Office of the Secretary. Beginning with the 1970 statistics, they are issued from the Department of Transportation, Federal Railroad Administration with the title *Carload Waybill Statistics*.

4. ——, Bureau of Accounts. *Freight Commodity Statistics, Class I Railroads in the United States for the Year Ended December 31, ——*.

   Origins of rail freight by district, commodity and breakdown by lines.

VI. Waterways

1. American Waterways Operators, Inc. *Inland Waterborne Commerce Statistics for the Calendar Year ——*.

   Ton-miles of various commodities carried on principal waterways.

2. U.S. Army Corps of Engineers. *Waterborne Commerce of the United States. Calendar Year ——*.

   Gives ton-miles of various commodities carried by vessel type and port for large U.S. regions.

3. U.S. Interstate Commerce Commission, Bureau of Accounts. *Transport Statistics in the United States, Part 5: Water Carriers*.

   Gives financial statistics for individual carriers, and a commodity breakdown by navigation areas for maritime and inland carriers.

4. U.S. Maritime Administration. *Domestic Oceanborne and Great Lakes Commerce of the United States*. Annual.

   Gives commodity breakdown of origins and destinations for navigation areas and large ports.

   For a discussion of waterborne commerce statistics, see W.A.C. Connelly, "Statistics on Waterborne Commerce compiled by the Corps of Engineers, U.S. Army," in *Highway Research Record No. 82, Freight Transportation – 9 Reports*, Publication 1267, (Washington: National Academy of Sciences–National Research Council, 1965).

VII. Statistical Studies

1. Burstein, M. L., A. Victor Cabot, John W. Egan, Arthur P. Hurter and Stanley L. Warner. *The Cost of Trucking: Econometric Analysis*. Dubuque, Iowa:

William C. Brown Co. for the Transportation Center at Northwestern University, 1965.

This book analyzes how trucking costs vary with firm size.

2. Meyer, John R., Merton J. Peck, John Stenason, Gerald Kraft, and Robert Brown. *Avoidable Costs of Passenger Train Service.* Report prepared by a Research Committee of the Aeronautical Research Foundation, Cambridge, Massachusetts, 1957.

   This article presents a brief but complete discussion of passenger train costs.

3. Oi, Walter Y. and Arthur P. Hurter, *Economics of Private Truck Transportation.* Dubuque, Iowa: William C. Brown Co. for the Transportation Center at Northwestern University, 1965.

   This book discusses all of the elements which enter into trucking costs; for example, how costs vary with length of haul, truck size and load.

4. Systems Analysis and Research Corporation. *The Cost of Air Cargo Service.* Report prepared for the Civil Aeronautics Board, June, 1962.

   This two-volume report analyzes air freight costs, and presents briefly much of the theoretical economic background to such cost studies.

The most complete single cost study is Meyer et al., *The Economics of Competition in the Transportation Industries* (I.E.10), which analyzes the costs of each mode. Part II of Meyer et al., *The Urban Transportation Problem* (I.E.12) analyzes the comparative costs of alternative urban transportation technologies.

About the Authors

Gerald Kraft is president of Charles River Associates. He is the author of "New Directions for Passenger Demand Analysis and Forecasting," *Transportation Research* (Vol. I, No. 3, 1967, with Martin Wohl); "Estimation of Urban Passenger Travel Behavior: An Economic Demand Model," *Highway Research Record,* No. 238 (1968, with Thomas A. Domencich and Jean-Paul Valette); *Free Transit* (Lexington, Mass., D.C. Heath and Company, 1970, with Thomas A. Domencich); and many other works on transportation economics. He is a panel member of the Maritime Transportation Research Board, National Academy of Science, and has consulted on many projects involving both transportation and regional economics. Mr. Kraft did undergraduate work at Wayne State University and graduate work in economics at Harvard University.

John R. Meyer is professor of economics at Yale University and president of the National Bureau of Economic Research. He is the author of *Economics of Competition in the Transportation Industries* (Cambridge: Harvard University Press, 1959, with M. J. Peck, C. Zwick, and J. Stenason), *The Urban Transportation Problem* (Cambridge: Harvard University Press, 1965, with M. Wohl and J. Kain), *Techniques of Transport Planning* (Washington: The Brookings Institution, 1971, with D. Kresge, M. Straszheim, and P. Roberts), and many other books and articles on economic and statistical problems. He is a consultant to the Council of Economic Advisers, The U.S. Department of Housing and Urban Development, and Department of Commerce, and has served on numerous advisory boards and panels. Professor Meyer is a director of Charles River Associates. He did undergraduate work at the University of Washington and received the Ph.D. in economics from Harvard University.

Jean-Paul Valette holds a Ph.D. in economics from the University of Colorado. He is the author of "Estimation of Urban Passenger Travel Behavior: An Economic Demand Model." *Highway Research Record,* No. 238 (1968, with Thomas A. Domencich and Gerald Kraft) and *Silver: An Industry Analysis* (Lexington, Mass.: D.C. Heath and Company, forthcoming, with James C. Burrows and William R. Hughes). Mr. Valette is an applied economist with expertise in transportation, pollution, and metals industries.